Contribution of Bal Gangadhar Tilak to Indian Socio-Political Thoughts

Author

Dr. Kusum Lata

AkiNik Publications
New Delhi

Published By: *AkiNik Publications*

AkiNik Publications
169, C-11, Sector - 3,
Rohini, Delhi-110085, India
Toll Free (India) – 18001234070

Author: *Dr. Kusum Lata*

The author/publisher has attempted to trace and acknowledge the materials reproduced in this publication and apologize if permission and acknowledgements to publish in this form have not been given. If any material has not been acknowledged please write and let us know so that we may rectify it.

1st Edition: *2018*

Pages: *108*

ISBN: *978-93-5335-044-4*

Price: *₹649/-*

Preface

"Liberty is the life-breath of a nation; and when the life is attacked, when it is sought to suppress all chance of breathing by violent pressure, any and every means of self preservation becomes right and justifiable" were the fiery motivating words of Father of Indian Unrest Bal Gangadhar Tilak, which aroused a sleeping nation to action from his views, making Indians aware of their plight under an imperialist rule.

The Indian National Congress, from its inception in 1885, was dominated by western educated Indians who believed in the philosophy of liberalism. They believed in gradual progress that was to be accomplished through the goodwill and sympathy of the British Empire. Hence, they insisted on constitutional methodology. But the younger generation of educated Indians rejected the entire thinking of the former generation raised a call for Swaraj or independence for the nation. The elder leaders of the Congress were shocked by the attitude of the nationalists youth and they named them 'Extremists' and dubbed their beliefs as 'Extremism'. Popularly known Lal Bal Pal, Lala Lajpat Rai, Bal Gangadhar Tilak, and Bipan Chandra Pal led the group of young nationalists and the trio contributed to the development of nationalist thought and movement in India.

About the Book

This volume presents a critical assessment of the political philosophy of Lokmanya Bal Gangadhar Tilak. Providing rich insight into his life and achievements, it analyses the politico-social situation and factors that shaped his ideology and perception. It also deals with his concept of Swaraj, his social philosophy and legacy.

Coverage and Structure

Divided into five chapters, the present book brings out the contribution of prominent nationalist leader Lokmanya Bal Gangadhar Tilak to Indian Political Thoughts in the British era.

Chapter 1, *Life and Activities* gives life sketch and view of political journey of Lokmanya Bal Gangadhar Tilak in Indian history, highlights as to how Tilak appeared on the political front in India when the moderates were dominating the politics of India.

Chapter 2, *Social Philosophy of Tilak,* tries to find out the relevance of Tilak ideas to the today's society. An attempt has been made to trace out the weaknesses and positive aspects of social philosophy of Tilak.

Chapter 3, Political Ideas of Tilak, *tries to interpret the personality and evaluate the accomplishments of Tilak against the background of Indian Nationalism.*

Chapter 4, *Concept of Swaraj,* tries to examine the expansion of the idea of freedom in the Western and Indian thought. This chapter brings to light the various aspects of the concept of swaraj in the writings of Bal Gangadhar Tilak.

Chapter 5, *Conclusion, concludes the contents of the present writings.*

Acknowledgements

This book would not have been possible without the support of a number of people.

I acknowledge the contribution of my teachers, students, and colleagues, whose queries and discussions helped me crystallize my thoughts on the political life of Lokmanya Bal Gangadhar Tilak.

My daughter, Shikha, has been a constant source of help with her advice, proofreading, conceptual inputs, and constructive criticism. I also express my gratitude towards my parents and family, who showed tremendous support during my long hours of work.

The constant encouragement and continuous support of my friends also helped me in bringing this long process of writing to an end.

Thank you all for your help in shaping my efforts.

Kusum Lata

Contents

Chapter - 1

Life and Development of Thought of Tilak

Bal Gangadhar Tilak was born in a middle class Chitpavan Brahmin family of moderate means in the Ratnagiri district of Konkan on the west coast of India on 23rd July, 1856. It was just one year before the first war of Indian Independence. His father, Gangadhar Pant was a teacher by profession and a Sanskrit scholar. He was also very proficient in Mathematics. Tilak's mother Parwatibai, was a pious lady. She played a critical role in building his firm character and taught him the values of India's classical heritage. From his teacher-father he inherited his love for Sanskrit, which gave him a deep insight into the ancient religion and tradition of the country and its people. Young Tilak was thus brought up in an atmosphere of orthodoxy and traditions. According to D.P. Karmarkar,

"Tilak's way of life in college was of orthodox type. He used to sit for meals with a silk dhoti as was common among orthodox Hindus and his outlook in social matters also was more conservative than others." [1]

His father Gangadhar was transferred to Pune from Ratnagiri as an Assistant Deputy Educational Inspector when he was ten years of age. This provided him with an opportunity to get higher education. He joined the Anglo-Vernacular School in Pune. Soon after coming to Pune Tilak lost his dear mother Parwatibai on July 24, 1866. Tilak was married in 1871. In 1872, his father died and in the same year Tilak completed his matriculation.

In 1873, Tilak joined the Deccan College. In those days he began living in one of the college hostel. When Tilak joined the college he found that his physical structure was not robust. Hence he decided to devote the first year of his college life only of making his physique vigorous, hence he failed his examination in the B. A. Examination. But he passed the next year. While a student at the Deccan College Tilak went for one term, in 1875, to the Elphinstone College, Bombay. The teacher of Mathematics there was Mr. Hawthormwait. Tilak was not satisfied with the teaching of mathematics at the Eiphinstone College, hence, he returned back to the Deccan College.

In 1876, after completing his graduation in the first division, Tilak appeared at the M.A. Examination in Mathematics but he failed. Then he dropped the idea of getting M.A Degree and finally he studied law from 1877 to 1879 so that he could serve his nation in a better way, by equipping himself with knowledge of jurisprudence. He specialized in Hindu law. While he studying Hindu law, he read almost all the important works on Hinduism, including the Sanskrit commentaries. [2] Tilak, like every other educated person, could have secured a Government job, but he preferred to serve the society independently and took to journalism in 1880.

During the 1880's Tilak became involved in a series of nationalistic endeavours, notably in the formation of New English School (1880) and Deccan Education Society (1884)

The school and society were founded on the missionary principles of self-sacrifice and selfless work [2], but within a few years serious difference emerged concerning the interpretation of these ideas. The immediate contention was whether life members of the society should have employment outside the society and whether they should contribute such income to the society. The quarrels culminated in the resignation of Tilak from the Deccan Education Society.

In 1881, Tilak and five others established the 'Mahratha' and 'Kesari' newspapers - the former was published in English and the later in Marathi. The primary objective of Tilak and his colleagues was to impart national education in order to create national consciousness. Mahratha kept in view the more advanced portion of the community.

Through his writings in the Kesari, he tried to make the people conscious of their rights. In his writings, Tilak very often invoked the tradition and history of Maharashtra. These writings made him very popular among his populace. Later Agarkar took charge of the Kesari and Tilak was responsible for the Mahrahha. But the journals remained the joint responsibility of their founders. Tilak did not concern himself with the Kesari except for topics like law and religion assigned to him. However, Tilak and Agarkar developed certain differences in their approach towards the question of social reforms. Agarkar felt so deprived of the opportunity of self-expression that he severed his connection from the Kesari in 1887. Tilak became the editor of the Kesan in place of Agarkar. In 1888, Agarkar started a new journal of his own — the Sudharak (Reformer) Tilak played a very important role to awaken and enlighten the masses through the Kesari and the Mahratha.

Tilak was a great writer in every sense of the term yet, oddly enough, he was a writer who disliked writing. Most of his journalistic essays were dictated by him and therefore his articles read like speeches. This fact served to increase their effectiveness, for when his views on heated issues were read to groups in the villages - this was the usual way of spreading the message of his newspapers - people accepted them as if Tilak was speaking to them in person. His style was always direct and his sentences short and crisp. His writings were crystal - clear and went straight to the heart of his readers. They were full of quotations from the ancient Sanskrit works, popular sayings, historical parallels, apt metaphors and, above all, pregnant with forceful and original ideas. [4]

His work, The Orion or Researches into the Antiquity of the Vedas was published in 1893. In this work he argued that the Rig Veda was composed as early as 4500 B.C. This thesis brought him recognition in the Western World. In, The Arctic Home in the Vedas, which was published in 1903, he asserted that the Aryans originally lived in the far northern reaches of the Asiatic Continent.

Tilak also organized Ganapati festival and Shivaji festival in 1896 to arouse in the people a sense of corporate feelings and political awakening which became a national festival onwards. In 1896 Maharastra was struck with famine. After the famine, the Government had brought out the Famine Relief Code and the famine situation had to be handled in accordance with the provisions contained therein. [5] Tilak translated the Famine Code into Marathi and made people conscious of their rights during the famine. At the end of the year, plague out in Bombay and Poona, Tilak (who was then an elected member of the Bombay Legislative Council) campaigned against the collection of land tax. [6]

Tilak wrote in the Kesari (January 12, 1897): "For the last twelve years we have been shouting (ourselves) hoarse, desiring that the Government should hear us. But our shouting has no more affected the Government than the sound of a gnat. Our rulers disbelieve our statements or profess to do so. Let us now try to force our grievances into their ears by strong constitutional means. We must give the best political education possible to the ignorant villagers. We must meet them on terms of equality teach them their rights and show how to fight constitutionally. Then only will the Government realize that to despise the Congress is to despise the Indian nation. Then only will the efforts of the Congress leaders be crowned with success. Such a work will require a large body of able and single minded workers, to whom politics would not mean some holiday recreation, but an everyday duty to be performed with strictest regularity and utmost capacity [7].

For the first time a leader had tried to educate the peasantry, mobilize it and to prepare it to fight against natural calamities and official injustice. The struggle launched by Bal Gangadhar Tilak was strictly constitutional. Tilak asked the Government to act upon the provisions for famine relief which were already on the statute book. The Kesari newspaper firmly and purposefully guided the agitation.

Tilak urged the starving populace to refuse to pay taxes. The activities of the agents of the Sarvajanik Sabha, who were engaged in famine relief work, were banned by the British Government and even prosecutions were launched against the more active workers. Despite these harassments Tilak and his colleagues carried on their propaganda.

This very agitation soon forced the Government to implement the Famine Relief Code. A Famine Fund was also established in Britain. Tilak's famine relief activities were doubly useful. In seeking economic redress he also carried political awakening of the grassroots of the country.

"While Tilak was thus engaged in the struggle for the amelioration of the agricultural classes, he had to plunge himself into another vortex to save the people from a visitation which followed in the wake of the fetid famine. Plague broke out in the Bombay Presidency" [8]. Tilak had to devote his attention to the bubonic plague in 1897 next to the efforts of the Government to control it. The anti-plague measures of the foreign Government created greater terror in the mind of public than the epidemic itself.

The plague spread first in Bombay and then in Poona in the state of Maharastra. Its mortality was very high. People fled away in panic from their native places and thus spread the epidemic. On 4th February, 1897, under the Epidemic Diseases Act the district magistrates were invested with powers to cope up with the situation. This Act gave powers to the authorities to detain steamer passengers and cargo, to examine railway passengers and to remove those affected to hospitals. Any home could be searched and any person segregated. The last two provisions of the Act caused distress and anger in plague affected Poona city.

Lokmanya in the beginning adopted an attitude of cooperation with the authorities but his voice tone changed because of the increased stupidity of the anti-plague operations under Rand, who was appointed Chairman of the Plague Committee.

Tilak set up a private hospital and opened a fund for relief in order to restore public confidence. Many prominent persons left Poona in panic of plague but Tilak remained in the city actively helping the needy and distressed. He criticized the Government for the barbarous methodology it was following and also criticized the public leaders for their apathy and inactivity.

The autocratic measures of Rand, the chairman of Plague Committee continued even after it was notified that the Plague had subsided and that inspection of homes would be discontinued. The cases of plague were still occurring. But Bal Gangadhar Tilak was ordered to close his sanatorium. He made an appeal to the higher authorities and the order was rescinded.

Lokamanya's humanitarian deeds during the plague were very significant. They revealed him to be a constructive political genius of the highest order. To set up the Hindu Plague Hospital in those days was a solid accomplishment because the spirit of public work was still dormant in India, and the grim devastation brought by the famine was still creating havoc for the populace. Some of the opponents of Tilak used to criticize him as an obstinate figure who relished destruction. But while such reckless critics were sitting idle or had left the city of Poona in terror of the disease, Tilak showed the expansiveness of his soul and his perfect faith in the teachings of the Hindu scriptures which he inherited from his family by not moving from the particular station which highest call of human duty had fixed for him. Here was the Karmayogi working in a spirit of Godward surrender for the realization of what the Gita called Lokasamsraha. The spirit of self-sacrifice was the highest criterion of spirituality. Spirituality did not mean isolation and de-individualization It meant the transcendence of egoistic interests and required self-immolation for the cause of mankind The heroic figure of Lokmanya Tilak ready to risk death and disaster in the plague and not fleeing from Poona exhibited the qualities of Karmayogi in a true sense.

That dark period in the history of Maharashtra served one purpose very well. It provided a crushing reply to all those do-nothing politicians and other arm-chair critics who, from a convenient shelter, always took sordid delight in taunting Tilak with being only destructive in his activities. Tilak's conduct during famine and plague of his times proved beyond the shadow of a doubt, that he was not merely a destructive critic but a constructive statesman of a high repute. His anti-plague measures with respect to Government's policy show constructive suggestions. Besides these healthy suggestions, Tilak tried his level best to prove them practically and he succeeded. He started a hospital providing maximum facilities to the people which proved exemplary rather than the Government hospital. It was not a minor achievement in those days. People were frightened out of their sense. Money was scarce owing to the famine and an insurmountable orthodoxy was rising. While his opponents had fled away from the city out of fear and were exhibiting their bravery only by means of their attacks from a safe distance against Tilak he undaunted by the plague was living and moving in the plague-affected areas without having any thought of risk for his own life only for the noble cause of providing relief to his unfortunate brethren Though the dire regime of the plague and the remedies against it had nearly ended it was replaced by an another dilemma i.e. the murder of Mr. Rand and Lt Ayerst in Poona [9].

The crime shocked the public and it made the Government virtually lose its head. Damodar Chaphekar was arrested and hanged. Tilak was shocked as much by the murder as by its aftermath. Even the attempts were made to implicate Tilak personally in the murder. Lokamanya was arrested in Bombay on July 27, 1897 after the murder of Rand and Ayerst in Poona on June 22, 1897. There was apparently no connection between these two events [10]. He was arrested on the charges of causing disaffection among the people against the Government by his writings in Kesari [11] and his public activities under section 124-A of the Indian Penal Code and was sentenced to eighteen months' rigorous imprisonment by the Session Court. This first sedition imprisonment endeared him to people. He was released on September 6, 1898.

The year 1889 was a landmark in the career of Tilak. In this year he attended the annual session of the Indian National Congress for the first time [12]. The Indian National Congress had been in the forefront of India's struggle for independence. It was the organization which nurtured India's advance towards nationalism [13]. Indian National Congress came into being in 1885. It had the privilege of associating with itself prominent persons like Hume, Raja Ram Mohan Roy, W.C. Bannerjee and many others. Tilak's name in the Congress appeared for the first time in 1889. Despite being an ardent advocate of Indian National Congress from its beginning and having attended and actively participated in its several sessions, Tilak could never occupy the Congress Presidential Chair. His name was suggested twice for that post but he could not adorn it for various reasons.

Tilak played an important role in various sessions of Indian National Congress. The Poona Congress of 1895 was significant because prior to this session of Congress, intense antagonism had aroused among the political leaders of Maharashtra. The basic question was whether the social conference should be allowed to use the Pandal of Congress. Tilak and his party felt that the Congress was a national organization and in no way it should become associated with a programme of social reform. Ultimately, it was decided not to allow social conference in the Congress Pandal [14].

In 1901 Congress, Tilak along with Lala Lajpat Rai attempted to build up political opinion against the then Congress because it was dominated by Pherozeshah Mehta and the moderates. The partition of Bengal came in 1905. Tilak visited different parts of the country and called upon the people to get ready for the struggle for freedom. This was the year when Tilak emerged as the national leader, an uncompromising champion of swaraj. He rejected the moderate policy of prayer and petition and along with other extremists started four fold political programme of swaraj, swadeshi, boycott and national education.

Tilak attended the Banaras session of the Congress in 1905. For the first time in a Congress meeting he announced that India must have swaraj. Tilak told the nation that there would be political boycott and political Swadeshi for the goal of swaraj - whether the moderates agreed or not.

The Banaras Congress approved of the active measures of swadeshi and boycott employed by Bengal and showed that Congress was prepared to move with the times [15]. In this session of Congress, it was proved that there was an underlying current of nationalism which could not be suppressed and that the battle lines were being drawn. Tilak and the nationalists had declared a state of non-violent war with the bureaucracy, and if need be with those who would support the bureaucracy. The leadership of the moderates now understood that they and the nationalists disagreed on both means and objectives. The moderates therefore began to prepare to meet an active nationalist front at the next session of the congress in 1906 [16]. Lokamanya attended the Calcutta Congress in 1906.

The passing of the boycott and swadeshi resolution at Calcutta session of the Indian National Congress indicated the growing political ascendancy of Tilak.

He attended the Surat session of the Congress in 1907, which was a very crucial session because Congress was broken at Surat Session of Congress. In this session, the moderates had proposed the name of Rash Behari Ghosh for the Presidentship of the Congress. The Nationalists had proposed the name of Lala Lajpat Rai who had just then been released, and whose election as President of the Congress would have effectively shown the nation's disapproval of his deportation without a trial. But the vital question over which controversy was certain was the resolution on Swadeshi and boycott. Tilak and the nationalists wanted the Congress to set its seal of approval on Swadeshi and boycott by reiterating its faith in these as the approved and legitimate means of winning Swarajya. The negotiations between the two parties took an unfavourable turn when the long delayed list of the draft resolutions omitted altogether the resolution on Swadeshi and boycott. This list which had to be submitted fully a month before the date of the session of the Congress, was presented in the afternoon of the 26th December, the opening day of the session. This irritated Tilak as the moderate leaders seemed to be bent on doing the work of drafting the resolution without any reference to the Nationalists On the first day of the Congress session Rao Bahadur Ambalal Desai stoop up to propose Ghosh to the chair As soon as he had started his speech the peace of the pandal was broken by shouts and countershouts [17]. During the night there was much activity to bring about a compromise, but no further information regarding the resolutions came forth and Tilak made up his mind to oppose the motion for the election of Ghosh by proposing a further adjournment to explore possibilities of a compromise. By the appointed time the pandal was filled to capacity. Surendranath Bannerjee supported the motion of Ghosh's election as President. The audience gave him a peaceful hearing. At the end of Banerjee's speech Ghosh proceeded to take the Presidential chair and Tilak mounted on to the rostrum to move his amendment. Tilak told him that he had come up to move an amendment to the motion of his election and that he had not been duly elected. There were shouts in favour of and against Tilak. Just then a chair was hurled at him and held by a Punjabi delegate in the course of its flight. In a few minutes the Police appeared on the scene and gently but firmly cleared the pandal [18]. Thus the difference between the moderates and the extremists led to a split in the Congress at its session held in 1907 at Surat However the efforts which were being made since 1907 to unite the two wings of the Congress succeeded in the Lucknow session of the Congress in 1916.

Tilak and extremists were a danger to British rule. Hence, the Government was bent upon penalizing Tilak. The cult of the bomb[19] which made its appearance in Bengal on April 30, 1908, was responsible for his arrest two months later [20]. He was arrested on June 24, 1908. The complaint against him was regarding the articles entitled, "the country's misfortune" and these remedies are not lasting, published in the Kesari. Tilak was titled by a special jury and was fined Rs. 1000.00 and ordered six years transportation to Mandalay.

Lokamanya reached Mandalay on September 23. During his stay at Mandalay he wrote the Gita Rahasya which is one of the fine works on the philosophy of Karamyoga. It is not merely a book on metaphysics based on intellectual dialectics and disquisitions, but is the revelation of the worldview and message of a great Rishi of modern India. The noble and pure living of Tilak enlightens the message of his book [21].

Tilak was released in June, 1914. His release provided the opportunity for the incorporation of a vital and dynamic force into Indian politics. The First World War broke in August, 1914. Lokamanya made a historical pronouncement of his policy at this critical moment. He praised the Morley-Minto Reforms. He criticized the acts of violence and terrorism that had been taking place in India and promised help to the Government in its hour of need.

The Bombay session of the Congress (1915) made an amendment to the Congress Constitution providing for an "election of delegates to the Congress from any public body irrespective of whether it was registered or not" [22]. Lokamanya decided to take advantage of this opening and in January, 1916, he publically stated that the nationalist party would re-enter the Congress. Tilak's re-entry into Congress symbolized the dawn of a new vitality in the politics of the country.

The formation of the Home Rule League[23] was the crowning achievement of Tilak's political career. A conference of nationalists was held in Poona in 1915 to discuss the desirability of establishing a Home Rule League. The conference was a great success and Tilak played a pivotal role in this conference. Home Rule League was established in April 28, 1916 at Belgaum to prepare the country for swaraj. Annie Besant founded the Home Rule League for Madras on the 3rd September, 1916. The two Home Rule Leagues under Tilak and Annie Besant began to play a revitalizing political role. They gave a broad basis to the nationalist movement. The whole of western India began to pulsate with a new political spirit. The spell of Tilak's personality was so great that Shaukat Ali pointed out that he and his brother who were interned in Chindwara became members of Home Rule League.

Initially, the movement was confined to press and public meetings. As it permeated among the masses, Government became more and more repressive [24]. The Government instituted a security case against Tilak under section 108 of the Criminal Procedure Code, for three speeches [25] delivered by him on Home Rule. However, Tilak obtained a ruling from the Bombay High Court that the demand for Home Rule was not seditious. Ultimately, Tilak was freed of the charges. This decision of the Bombay High Court restored to Tilak his liberty of speech. He concentrated his energies on the spread of the Home Rule Movement.

In October, 1916, a joint meeting of the League Council and the All India Congress Committee was held. At this meeting an agreement was arrived at between them. "According to the Congress - League scheme the

Moslems agreed to self government and the Congress agreed to communal electorates for the Moslems" [26]. This acceptance of the Congress-League scheme was primarily due to the influence exercised by Lokamanya Tilak. He played a decisive role in the Lucknow Congress of 1916. A resolution of self-government was passed in this Congress and the Congress accepted the Congress-League Scheme in this session.

Lokamanya was engaged in political activities after the Lucknow Congress. During 1917 and 1918, he carried on intensive propaganda work for the Home Rule. The growing agitation carried on by the Home Rule Leagues necessitated some pronouncement by British Government. Montagu the Secretary of State for India, declared on August 20, 1917 that the policy of British Government was that of the increasing association of Indians in every branch of the administration and the gradual development of self-governing institutions with a view to the progressive realization of responsible government in India as an integral part of the British Empire. Tilak welcomed the announcement as making an advance in the right direction even though it was unsatisfactory both in language and substance.

Lokamanya was accorded an extra-ordinarily magnificent and royal welcome at the Calcutta Congress of 1917. He made powerful speeches on self-government and on the issue of the release of Ali-brothers. The Calcutta Congress passed a historic resolution about the national demand for selfgovernment. Tilak supported this resolution. "At the Calcutta Congress, Tilak appeared as a tower of strength not only to the nationalists but to the country as a whole" [27].

Tilak proceeded to England in September 1918 for his suit of defamation against Sir Valentine Chirol, the Director of the Imperial Department of the London Times. Chirol had contributed a series of articles on the explosive political situation in India and afterwards in 1910 published those articles, based mainly on the Government records, in a book form under the title The Indian Unrest. He called Tilak in that book as 'Father of Indian Unrest', and attempted to establish his relations with revolutionaries in India. In his opinion, Tilak was the inspirer and perhaps organizer too of the outbursts of bomb and secret societies especially in Bengal. Tilak was in the Mandalay jail when the book was published so he could not contradict statements contained therein. After his release in June 1914, Tilak filed the suit of libel on Chirol in October 1915. Owing to various obstructions of the Government, he could not sail to England till September, 1918.

Tilak was anxious to vindicate not only his own character but also the cause of Indian freedom. What he particularly objected to was Chirol's interpretation of his writings and speeches as incitement to political murders. Chirol held Lokamanya responsible in some way or other [28].the machinery of the Government was geared to help Chirol. Therefore, Tilak lost the case against Chirol.

Tilak's stay in England caused no small amount of strain on the intelligence department of the British Government. His activities were very carefully watched. The Government of India had deputed its own staff which sent weekly reports on Tilak and his colleagues. They (the Tilak party) had neutralized, in a large measure, the effect of the Indo-British Association. They had made a number of labour leader's champions of the Indian cause. It was now certain that the impression left on the minds of intelligent and sympathetic Englishmen would not easily be altered by Indian moderate arguments that self-government by stages was what India wanted [29].

"Tilak's activities in England were confined to public meetings and cultivating contacts with eminent Britishers. He also won the confidence of the British Labour Party. He extended his Home Rule campaign to America with the help of Lala Lajpat Rai. Within six months more than seventy organizations of Home Rule League were established in the U.S. with the Head Office in New York [30].

During his visit to England, Tilak was totally devoted to the cause of swaraj. He sailed back home on November 6, 1919. He attended the Amritsar Congress in 1919. Tilak gave the theory of responsive cooperation. He was willing to cooperate with government only to the extent that the government would be willing to cooperate with them. He argued, "We are prepared to cooperate, but if there is nothing to cooperate we shall not. It is almost a scandal to say that Indians are not prepared to cooperate for the sake of India... Let the authorities declare in what ways they are prepared to cooperate with us and we can assure them that if they cooperate with us, we can, with them. Cooperation is mutual" [31].

Lokamanya decided to form a party to fight the coming elections for capturing the legislatures as reformed by Montagu -Chelmsford Act in the month of March, 1920 during his tour to Sindh. The manifesto of the Congress Democratic Party was issued on 20th April, 1920. The Congress Democratic Party was mainly started for contesting elections and its activities and operations were confined to the Bombay Presidency. Tilak was the President of the Party. He wanted that a large number of nationalist members should be returned to the legislatures and they should reveal the inadequacies of the reforms Act of 1919 and should agitate for a more comprehensive legislation.

The manifesto of the Congress Democratic Party pledged its faith in the Congress and in Democracy. It believed that the growth of education and the extension of the franchise were necessary for the actualization of democracy. It recognized the tenant of religious toleration.

The merciless massacre of people at Jallianwala Bagh in 1919 led to the decision of non-cooperation movement. T.L. Shay argued that in view of these injustices, Gandhi felt that it was no longer possible for him to offer wholehearted co-operation to the British Raj. Gandhi now opposed the Congress presenting candidates for election to the Legislative Councils. He argued that non-cooperation be carried out in all spheres of life [32].

Tilak agreed, with reservations, that non-cooperation was a desirable programme. Gandhi was anxious to obtain Tilak's support. But Tilak disagreed with Gandhi on the question of Council entry. He believed that the more realistic attitude would be to enter the councils and their work tirelessly for swaraj, and if the nation followed non-cooperation, then conduct a non-cooperation campaign both within the Government and outside it [33]. Congressmen were waiting for Lokamanya in the special session of the Indian National Congress to be held at Calcutta in 1920. But 'Lion of India', Tilak could not reach. He died on 1st August, 1920.

The greatest Indian of his time had gone away to rest in God placing his countrymen securely on the path of Swarajya. Mr. Tilak had started his struggle for the attainment of Swarajya when even to think of Swarajya was a sin, to speak about it was sedition and to do anything for it was a revolt.

The Lokamanya had been the maker of a new era of democratic freedom based on the dignity and the rights of man, not only in Maharashtra but in the whole of India. With unswerving loyalty to his ideal of Independence for his country this fearless patriot and philosopher courted and suffered untold miseries and won a triumph over the adverse circumstances which surrounded him. His example is a guiding light to illuminate the path of those who decide to dedicate themselves to the service of their country seeking nothing for themselves except the great joy of labouring for others [34].

It was perhaps the destiny of India that Tilak should disappear from the scene after having aroused the strongest spirit of resistance to foreign rule and then Gandhi should usher in the form of resistance which would work and ultimately bring freedom to India [35]. The scene would had been different if Tilak and Gandhi had worked together for the cause of national freedom.

References

1. Karmarkar DP. Bal Gangadhar Tilak: A Study, Bombay, 1956, 30p.
2. Kelkar NC. Life and Times of Lokmanya Tilak, Trans, D.V. Divakar, Madras, S. Ganeshan, 1928, 57p.
3. *Ibid.,* 36p.
4. Tahmankar DV. Lokamanya Tilak: Father of Indian Unrest and Maker of Modern India (London: John Murray Publishers), 1956, 39p.
5. Varma VP. Life and Political Philosophy of Lokmanya Tilak, 81p.
6. Inamdar NR. "The Political Ideas of Lokmanya Tilak", in Thomas Pantham & Kenneth L. Deutsch, eds., Political Thought in Modern India (New Delhi: Sage Publications), 1986, 111p.
7. Quoted in Ram Gopal, Lokamanya Tdak: A Biography, 133p.
8. Dhananjay Keer, Lokanianya Tilak: Father of the Indian Freedom Struggle, 109 p.
9. Kelkar NC. Life and Times of Lokamanya Tilak, Trans. D.V. Divekar (New Delhi: Radha Publications), 2001, 360-61.
10. Jog NG. Lokamanya Bal Gangadhar Tilak, 64p.
11. There was incriminated two articles published m the Kesari of the 15th June, One was the report of his speech which he delivered on the occasion of the Shivaji festival. Another was a poem entitled Exhortations of Shivaji, 1897.
12. Varma VP. The Life and Philosophy of Lokamanya Tilak, 48p.
13. Vandana Talekar. Lokmanya Tilak and the Congress during 1885-1895, in Verinder Grover, *op. cit.,* 103p.
14. For details see Varma VP. The Life and Philosophy of Lokamanya Tilak, 74-78.
15. Bhat VG. Lokamanya Tilak: His Life, Mind, Politics and Philosophy (Poona: A Prakash Publication), 1956, 66p.
16. Theodore L Shay. The Legacy of Lokamanya: The Political Philosophy of Bat Gangadhar *Tilak*, 113p.
17. Bhat VG. Lokamanya Tilak: His Life, Mind, Politics and Philosophy, 76-77.
18. *Ibid,* 77-78.

19. At Muzaffarpur, Khudiram Bose and Prafulla Chaki threw a bomb with intention of killing kingsford, the District Judge. But the explosion actually killed European women. Its reactions were witnessed all over the country. The government sought to fight terrorism with counter-terrorism.
20. Jog NG. Lokamanya Bal Gangadhar Tilak, 115p.
21. Varma VP. The Life and Philosophy of Lokamanya Tilak, 321p.
22. Sumant YM. Tilak's Politics during 1914-20, in Verinder Grover, *op. cit.,* 142p.
23. Home Rule League was an organization started for educating public opinion and agitating for Home Rule. The League may be regarded as a pioneer movement and is not intended in sense to be an exclusive movement. Home Rule meant having the management of their home in their own hands.
24. Sumant YM. Tilak's Politics during 1914-20, in Verinder Grover, *op. cit.,* 144p.
25. On 31st May Tilak delivered the first speech on the home rule at Ahmednagar wherein he said that because the bureaucratic rule of the English imperialists was alien in its nature, hence there would be no sedition whatever nor any other offence in calling alien those things that were alien by nature. On June 1, 1916, he delivered the second speech on Home Rule at Ahmednagar. He exhorted the audience to get all the rights which belong to man by nature. On the 8"' October 1917, Tilak delivered another speech on home rule in the compound of the Home Rule League, Allahabad. He gave a logical analysis of the factors that led to the establishment of the Home Rule League. In this speech he also analyzed the concept of passive resistance, 1916.
26. Varma VP. The Life and Philosophy of Lokamanya Tilak, 356p.
27. *lbid,* 374p.
28. Jog NG. Lokamanya Bal Gangadhar Tilak, 156p.
29. Ram Gopal. Lokamanya Tilak: A Biography, 436p.
30. Sumant YM. Tilak's Politics during 1914-20 in Verinder Grover, *op.cit,* 144p.
31. Quoted in Athalye DV. The Life of Lokamanya. Tilak (Poona: Annasahib Chiploonkar), 1921, 294-95.

32. Theodore L Shay. The Legacy of Lokamanya: The Political Philosophy of Bal Gangadhar Tilak, 144p.

33. *Ibid.,* 144-45.

34. Bhat VG. Lokamanya Tilak: His Life, Mind, Politics and Philosophy, 113p.

35. Diwakar RR. The Lokamanya and the Mahatma, in Verinder Grover, *op. cit.,* 423p.

Chapter - 2

Social Philosophy of Tilak

Tilak was of the view that society was a divine creation. Man and society, according to him, were simultaneously created by God. He argued, "It is seen that in as much as the Paramesvara created man simultaneously with society, and society simultaneously with man" [1]. Tilak differed from the traditional individualists, who regarded society as a contrivance deliberately not up by man for the fulfilment of certain ends. He believed in the organic concept of society. He also believed that man was a social animal. To quote him, "we all have families and want to live within society. Under these circumstances, a compromise between the individual's wishes and society's expectations would have to be arrived at. Reforms accomplished through such compromise would come to stay. Those who want to live according to their own individual whims should do so on a desert island. Others who want to live in society will have to adopt a compromise" [2].

Tilak held that the nature of society was evolutionary. He differentiated between the imperfect society and the perfect society and argued that when all the individuals would realize the identity of the Atma in every created being perfect society would start. For this he prescribed that man should increase equability of reason which was possible by constant practice. His position became clear when he said, "One must always increase Equability of Reason by constant practice; and when the minds of all the human beings in the world gradually reach the state of perfect Equability in this way, Krtayuga will start, and the highest ideal or the most perfect state of human race will be reached by everyone" [3]. Thus, Tilak believed that individual could contribute in the development of society by his conscious efforts He said "Mind gentlemen that it lies mostly in your hands either to make or mar your future You are the architects of your own fortune" [4].

Tilak argued that for the welfare of the society and lokasamgraha (universal benefit) every individual should follow his dharm. Dharma meant the duty allotted to a person by the social arrangement. Lokamanya was of the view that dharma was necessary for the maintenance of society. To quote him, "when this dharma ceases to be observed, the binding ropes are loosened, society will be in the same position as the planetary system consisting of the Sun and the planets would be in the sky without the binding force of gravitation or as a ship would be on the ocean without a rudder" [5]. It is evident from this statement that Tilak gave importance to dharma for the maintenance of society. He held that it was important that artha and Kama should be acquired consistently with dharma without disturbing the arrangement of society.

The highest ideal for Tilak was the release of the soul (moksa). He argued, "Atmic benefit or metaphysical perfection is the first and the highest duty of everyman" [6]. He further said, "Although we accept maintenance of society as being the chief outward use of dharma, yet we never lose sight of the Redemption of the Atman (atman-kalyana) or Release (moksa) which is the highest ideal according to the Vedic or all other religions and which is the special feature of our view-point. Whether it is maintenance of society or the general material welfare of everybody, if these externally useful principles obstruct the redemption of the Atma, we do not want them" [7]. Thus Tilak regarded moksa to be the highest goal of everyman. According to him, perfection in this field was the first and foremost duty of man.

Tilak further said that every individual played an important role in the society. He argued, "Just as extremely small wheels are necessary along with large wheels in order that any machine should work properly, so also is it necessary that the authority of common-place persons should be exercised properly and fully in the same way as the authority of superior persons like Vyasa and others, in order that the immense and ponderous activity or mechanism of the cosmos should continue to work in a properly regulated manner" [8]. Here Tilak argued that persons from all walks of life were needed to run the society. Each and every person was important because everybody had a role to play in the society irrespective of their status, caste or creed.

He tried to harmonise the interest of individual with the interest of society by the principle of self-identification. He argued, "This easy principle of 'self-identification', (atmavpamya) which regulates the mutual behaviour of persons living in a society, is so comprehensive, so easy to understand, and so universally accepted, that when once one lays down the rule: Realise the identity of the Atman in all created beings, and behave towards others with an equable frame of mind, as if they are yourself, it is no more necessary to lay down such individual commandments as: be kind to others; help others as much as possible; bring about their welfare; put them on the path of advancement; love them; do not get tired of them; do not hurt their feelings; behave towards them with justice and equality; do not deceive any one; do not deprive any one of his wealth or of his life; do not tell anyone an untruth; bear always in mind the idea of bringing about the greatest good of the greatest number; behave towards all, looking upon them as the children of one and the same father, and as if they were your brothers etc" [9]. Tilak's principle of self-identification if followed can go a long way in bringing about harmony in society.

However, he argued that a person with an equable frame of mind could not follow the principle of self-identification in an absolute sense in an imperfect society. He further said that our religions do not preach that one should not give measure for measure and protect oneself. By performing such a retaliatory action non-inimically one does not commit a sin. Here, Tilak seems quite practical and realist.

He was opposed to the subordination of individual to individual or individual to society or society to society and said, "yet, as there is one and the same Atman in all created things, everyone has an inherent natural right of being happy in this world; and no single individual or society in the world can ever ethically acquire the right to cause the detriment of another individual or society by disregarding this universal, important, and natural light, merely because the one is more than other in numbers, or in strength, or because the one has a larger number of means than the other for conquering the other" [10]. He further said, "If someone seeks to justify the selfish conduct of a society, which is biggest in numbers than another society, on the ground that the benefit of a larger multitude, is of higher importance than the benefit of an individual or of a smaller multitude such a method of reasoning must be looked upon as demonical (raksasi)" [11]. Here he is trying to educate the big societies and powerful countries not to dominate smaller and weaker societies.

It is observed from the preceding discussion that Tilak was not consistent in his views on society. He regarded society as an organism. If society was an organism then individuals should belong to the society as parts belong to an organism. If we regard society as an organism the interest of society becomes more important than the interest of individuals. However, Tilak did not subordinate the individual to the society. He believed that every individual had the natural right of being happy and no one had a right to disregard that natural right of man. These two views were not consistent with each other.

No doubt, society is not a contrivance set up for limited ends. It can also not be denied that there is some resemblance between the functioning of a social system and that of an organism. There is an inter-dependence of individuals in society like the part of an organism. But it would not be correct to regard society an organism [12] because individuals have their own individuality and independent personality unlike the parts of an organism.

Tilak's contribution lied in emphasizing the predominant worth of the spiritual individual. In this respect he differed from western political idealists, like Plato, Hegel, Bradley and Bosanquet who gave more importance to the collectively.

He differed from the individualists in so far as the latter lay stress on individual ego and ignore the unity of individual with others in the society. Tilak believed that man could rise above ego. His idea of self-identification recognized unity of individual with others. He sought to reconcile the interest of the individual with the interest of the society on the basis of spiritualism and cosmopolitanism of Vedanta and ancient Indian thought.

In fact, he moved a step further and stressed harmony between individual, society and the universe. He highlighted unity between the interest of the individual and the interest of the world and said, "There is a fundamental unity underlying the Logos (Ishvara), man, and world. The world is in existence because the Logos has willed it so. It is His Will that holds it together" [13]. He further said, "Man strives to gain union with God; and when this union is achieved the individual will merges in the mighty universal will" [14]. He added, "If man seeks unity with the Deity, he must necessarily seek unity with the (interests) of the world also, and work for it. If he does not, then the unity is not perfect, because there is union between two elements out of the three (man and Deity) and the third (the world) is left out" [15]. Tilak held that serving the world, and thus serving His Will, was the surest way of salvation, and this way could be followed by remaining in the world and not going away from it.

Tilak was of the opinion that the doctrine of self-identification, in its widest sense, meant to identify oneself with the universe and to acquire the Vedantic vision of 'Vasudhaiva Kutumbakam'. He said that it could be achieved gradually. One should first of all identify oneself with the members of one's family by realizing that the Atman which was within oneself was also within the members of one's family and then one could make this self identification grow by substituting one's friends, one's relations, members of one's village or the members of one's community and finally all human beings and all created beings.

Thus Lokamanya talked about the development of the entire mankind into one family. In this respect he was inspired by the Vedantic Philosophy.

Writing on similar lines Aurobindo said, "The law for humanity is to pursue its upward evolution towards the finding and expression of the Divine in the type of mankind, taking full advantage of the free development and gains of all individuals and nations and groupings of men, to work towards the day when mankind may be really and not only ideally one divine family, but even then, when it has succeeded in unifying itself, to respect, aid and be aided by the free growth and activity of its individual and constituent aggregates" [16].

Lokamanya was influenced by Western liberal ideas and ancient Indian ideas in his views on the relationship between the individual and the society. He argued that every individual had an inherent natural right to be happy and no one had a right to cause harm to other. Tilak was influenced by the doctrine of natural rights which found expression in American and French Revolutions.

India was governed recklessly and despotically by the Britishers when Tilak emerged on the Indian political scene. The social structure of India was in a bad shape. The position of Indian masses was very grim. Illiteracy and ignorance were prevailing in the country. Indians were deprived of their rights by the foreign rule. Vinod Tiwari has argued that these situations deeply hurt Bal Gangadhar Tilak [17].

The society was divided into different castes. The people belonging to upper castes enjoyed special rights. The people of lower castes were treated as untouchables. They were not allowed to enter into the houses of the people of the upper castes. They were made to work for the benefits of the higher caste people. Not only this, many atrocities were hurled upon them. They were sometimes mercilessly beaten if they broke those norms which were set for them. The position of women in the Indian society was also grim. They were deprived of their rights. Widow re-marriage was not allowed in Hindu society Child marriages were encouraged at that time in India Sati system was another social evil prevalent in the Indian society we can say that Indian society was superstitious and backward in every sphere of life.

No doubt some movements were launched to reform the traditional Indian society. The reform movements represented the striving of the conscious and progressive sections of the Indian people to democratize social institutions and remodel old religious outlooks to suit the new social needs [18]. The movements strived towards abolition of caste system, equal rights for woman, a campaign against child marriage, sati system, against the ban on widow remarriage and against social and legal inequalities. These movements in varying degrees, tried to awaken and educate the masses against these social evils. Some of the reform movements like the Brahmo Samaj, the Prathana Samaj and Arya Samaj made an attempt to remove evils from the Indian society and tried to bridge the gulf between modern European rationalism and the traditional life and institutions of Indian people.

There were reformers like Dr. Bhao Daji of Bombay and Sardar Gopala Hari Deshmukha called the 'Hitavad' of Poona. They opposed the traditional monopoly of Brahmins. Other reformers who supported the movement for social emancipation were Dadoba Pondurang, Bal Gangadhar Jambhekar, Vaman Abaji Modak and Vishnu Parashman Shastri.

The social reforms were taken up by Gopal Ganesh Agarkar, Mahadev Govind Ranade, Kashinath Trimbak Telang, Ramkrishan Gopal Bhandarkar and Narayan Ganesh Chandavarkar in the 1880's in Maharashtra. T.L. Shay has argued that the interest in social reforms led many westernized intellectuals to an interest in politics. In trying to enact and realize some of their reform schemes, many sought a voice in political affairs, aspiring to It was founded by Raja Ram Mohan Roy in 1828. It was founded in 1867. "It was founded in Bombay in 1875 by Swami Dayanand bring about moderate political reforms. Thus, the extremists in social reform became the moderates of political reform [19].

They were representatives of the uprooted intellectuals and emerging middle class. They did not represent the masses of India. They were of the view that political reforms would gradually be bestowed as a gift from the British regime. They tended to direct their most severe criticism not against the British rule but against the traditional institutions of the Indian system of social order. They wanted to induce the British Indian Government to take action to bring social reforms which they believed to be necessary in the making of India.

From 1885 to 1905, Indian National Congress was dominated by these moderates. A group of extremists emerged within the Congress and began to dominate Congress from 1905. Prominent among these leaders were Lala Lajpat Rai, Bipin Chandra Pal, Aurobindo Ghosh and Bal Gangadhar Tilak. They opposed the moderate's policy of prayers and petitions. They gave priority to political emancipation over the social reforms. They did not want to induce the British Indian Government to take action to bring social reforms. They were opposed to reforming Indian society on the western lines. T.L. Shay argues that these men were not satisfied with the western civilization's system of values; they were not prepared to reject India's own philosophy of life in order to imitate the philosophy of the British Empire. They believed that the forms of social order in India were in need of drastic reforms, but instead of judging Indian social practices by the standards of the West, they looked for their own standards within their own civilization [20].

Arguing on these lines Tilak said, "We have behind us a tradition in religion and knowledge. Our tradition in religion and knowledge is equal, nay, even superior to those possessed by others. If we gave up these traditions, then we shall be devoid of any ties that will bind our people together. To break the time-honoured traditions is to break the spirit of the people who hold them. We should constantly bear these things in mind" [21].

On a superficial analysis, Tilak does not seem to be very consistent in his attitude towards social reforms. He was against the Age of Consent Bill [22] however he did not marry his daughters until they were sixteen. He argued that he was not against the social reforms but he did not want Congress to become associated with a programme of social reforms. He argued that he was against untouchability but refused to sign the manifesto for the removal of untouchability. This has led scholars to form different opinions regarding his views on social reforms. Stanley A. Wolpert has argued that in Tilak "social reaction served as the handmaid of political revolution, though the latter was often as revivalist in aim as the former was conservative in impulse [23].

Tilak has been blamed for not criticizing the existing social order rather it is argued that he defended the defective social system. Dhananjay Keer said, "It is unfortunate to note that he never raised his little finger against the existing social order which was sagged with injustice and inequality and misery. Had he assumed at least the role of neutrality in matters social, he would have indirectly contributed to the progressive social forces that were working for the reorganization of society on deeper and broader foundations. But instead of widening the mental horizon of the orthodox and helping the development of new social attitudes, he defended the defective and decaying institutions of that old social order with unabated ferocity. Not only did he do this but also he led an active, bitter opposition to the social reform movement and helped the social reactionaries" [24]. Dhananjay Keer further said that he did not look at the non-Brahmin problem. To quote him "Tilak failed to look at the non-Brahmin problem from the angle of social justice and equality, its basic urge for a better social order in a changing age and the needs of a changing social and economic life. And his talks to the non-Brahmins, which were of a condescending and patronizing rather than democratic nature, amply proved that he could not outgrow, as sometimes great men do, the social barriers under which he was born. It is just like the tragedy in the life of Churchill who fought for democracy and human freedom and yet turned down India's demand for freedom and equality and justice" [25].

N.C. Kelkar said that even his sons, who held progressive views in social matters, jokingly told Tilak that they did not want to be Lokamanya as they thought that their father's title rested much on his orthodox views [26].

Tilak was criticized by the social reformers like Ranade, Gopal Krishan Gokhale, Bhandarkar, Byramji Malabari, Agarkar and others, for being reactionary in social matters because of certain reasons. Firstly, the 'Age of Consent Bill' was introduced by Sir Andrew in the Imperial Legislative Council at Calcutta on the 9th January, 1891. Tilak opposed the bill. On the 20th January, 1891, he argued in the Kesari that the proposed bill was bound to interfere in Hindu religion and hence the people were exhorted to oppose the passage of the bill. Though Tilak did not succeed in getting the bill rejected, still he emerged as a leader of opposition to the Government and to the group of social reformers. Secondly, 4th October, 1890 became an important day in the social history of Poena because forty-two persons including Tilak, Ranade and Gokhale had taken tea at the house of a missionary [27]. This incident originated the storm. The main mover in the affair was Gopalrao Joshi. He engineered through the Panch Howd Mission at Poona, an invitation to the leaders like Ranade, Tilak, Gokhale and others to deliver lectures at the mission. The leaders were served tea after the lectures were over, Hindu leaders taking tea publically at Christian house was in those days a monstrous idea. Tilak said that he would take tea if a Brahmnn served it. The brother of Gopalrao Joshi served them tea. The names of all these persons were published in a Poona weekly in January, 1891.

A case to the Ecclesastical Court of Shankaracharya was referred by Balasaheb Natu, the leader of the Sanatanists. Tilak argued that the Shastras prescribed prayacchitta for such occasions and by undergoing certain ceremonies people could become purified. On this account also he was labelled a social reactionary.

Thirdly, Ramabai, a baptized Christian started the Sharda Sadan as a home for widows in Bombay and later on at Poona. But she was suspected of spreading Christianity among the students. Lokamanya wrote in the Kesari, "Christian woman trying to infiltrate in our society under the clock of female education and their supporters however learned would be regarded by us as enemies of the people and of Hinduism" [28]. Though there was evidence to doubt Ramabai's bonafides, Tilak was dubbed by social reformers as an enemy of woman education [29]. Fourthly, in 1895 politics became embittered in Poona which had been selected as the venue of the year's National Congress. Prior to this session of the Congress antagonism had aroused among the political leaders of Maharashtra. Tilak and his supporters put forth a demand that the pavilion of the Poona Congress should not be allowed for the use of the Social Reform Conference. [30] While the opposite group demanded the use of the pandal for the social conference. For this reason also Tilak was branded as a social reactionary.

Fifthly, it was believed that Tilak's views regarding the question of untouchability and the depressed classes were of the orthodox type. He refused to sign the manifesto for the removal of untouchability [31]. This has led the scholars to form different opinions regarding his views on social reforms.

On the other hand Lokamanya has been regarded as a social revolutionary. N.C. Kelkar regarded him "a practical reformer" [32]. T.L. Shay called him as "an ardent advocate of social reform" [33], and D.V. Tahmankar argued that Tilak's "claim to be regarded as a social revolutionary is unchallengeable" [34].

There were certain specific issues, which prove that Lokamanya was not opposed to social reforms. Firstly, though Tilak opposed the 'Age of Consent Bill', he did not marry his daughters until they were sixteen. Moreover, he had formulated constructive proposals for social reforms. These proposals which show that he was not a reactionary are as follow: (1) Girls should not be married before the age of 16. (2) Boys should not be married before the age of 20. (3) No man should marry after he was 40. (4) If a man wanted to marry again he should marry a widow. (5) The use of liquor should be prohibited. (6) The system of dowry should be abolished. (7) Widows should not be tonsured. (8) Those who accepted these reforms should contribute one-tenth of the income to their promotion. Needless to say, none in the camp of the reformers came forward to support Tilak's proposals [35].

Some of the proposals of Tilak were very radical. It is evident from the fact that dowry was banned only in 1961 in India. However, we have not been able to remove this evil from our society. The prohibition is yet to be enforced throughout the country despite its being a Directive Principle of our Constitution. Child marriages are prevalent in various parts of the country.

No doubt, Tilak took a leading part in the controversy regarding the age of consent bill. He argued that the autonomy of Hindu society should not be disturbed by Governmental legislation. He said, "We would not like that Government should have anything to do with regulating our society customs or ways of living [36]. He added, "If we want that we should be proficient in the art of self-government, the first qualification we should show is the ability to manage our own business among ourselves, and particularly that business which will be better regulated by ourselves than by passing an act or resolution. If we want acts and resolutions to regulate child-marriage or widow marriage among us, why then we should have, 'Dinner Acts', 'Sandhya adoration Acts', 'Bathing time Acts', and so forth [37]. Tilak was against the Government interference in religious matters. Because according to him religion was a personal matter. He wanted the social and religious matters to be tackled by the society itself. According to him, a foreign bureaucracy had no right to sit in legislative judgement on the Indian society. To quote him "I did not think nor do I think now, that a legislature which is not wholly responsible to the public is competent to deal with social questions" [38].

It is observed that Tilak was against the Government interference in regulating the social reforms because it would had resulted in the increase of the power of the alien government over them. Therefore, he opposed the Age of Consent Bill.

Secondly, the controversy about the Panch Howd Mission Tea party and the dispute in the court of Shankaracharya showed Tilak's spirit of compromise. He would neither yield to the dictates of the extreme type orthodoxy nor would he throw overboard existing social customs. There is no doubt that he underwent the procedure laid down by Hindu scriptures. But if anybody took it into his head to taunt him with it, he was ready to prove that the mere sipping of tea, called for no such purification. He declared, "There was no sin in taking tea from anybody [39].

However, to pacify his angry followers, Tilak did undergo a sort of penance and there the episode ended. Here lay the fundamental difference between Tilak and other social reformers. He wanted to take the people with him and was therefore extremely careful not to hurt their religious feelings. He pointed out that social reformers would never succeed by ridiculing the age-old customs and habits of the people, which were hallowed by long practice and tradition [40].

When social reformers quoted the example of Luther, who reformed the Christians faith, he argued, "Luther succeeded because he believed and respected the tenants of Christianity. He did not flout the Bible. Let our reforming friends follow the great Christian leader and respect the Hindu scriptures and they will see a miraculous change in the attitude of the people [41]. It seems that Tilak wanted to take a leap forward in social reform without forsaking the people far behind and without bringing the religion of the forefathers into contempt or even into slight disrespect.

Thirdly, in Ramabai case, Tilak was blamed by the social reformers as an enemy of women's education. Tilak was not against the Sharda Sadan provided it confined itself to the work of imparting secular education. He had given education to his own daughters. He was not against the woman education and the emancipation of widows but he could not reconcile himself to the game of Christian conversion. Later on, Ramabhai's indulgence in proselytizing activities compelled Ranade and Bhandarkar to sever their connection with the Sharda Sadan thereby justifying the stand taken earlier by Tilak.

Fourthly, as far as the controversy about holding social conference in the Congress Pandal was concerned, Tilak argued that social conference should not be allowed to use the pavilion built for the Congress work. Stanley A. Wolpert has argued that in appealing for Congress funds to finance the preparations Tilak said that no one contributed money with the stipulation that the Social Conference should be allowed to use the same pandal [42]. According to Tilak, money collected for the National Congress would be spent only for the sake of Congress because the social conference was useless in the eyes of many people. He valued the successful holding of the Congress much more than that of social conference because the question of social reform could create divisive tendencies.

According to Tilak, "In view of the magnitude of the task that faces us; we have got to forget our petty differences. Remember, gentlemen that the interest of our motherland at this critical juncture requires that all of us should work hand in hand [43].

He argued that the mixing up of social reforms with that of Congress work was unfortunate. It was true that the issue of social reforms was very important in Indian renaissance but it could have an independent platform. He felt that Congress was a national organization and it should not become associated with a programme of social reforms, which was a controversial issue.

Here, Lokamanya talked about the concept of division of labour and argued that he was working for the political emancipation and some other people should take up the question of social reforms and of the depressed classes. He was fully devoted to the cause of National emancipation. V.P. Varma has argued that when somebody asked Tilak as to how was he prepared to go to England where it would be difficult to maintain orthodoxy in matters of food, Tilak told him that Maratha Brahmin were realists and could adjust with the situation for the sake of the country [44].

Fifthly, an in-depth analysis reveals that Tilak was not in favour of untouchability at all. The men of the lower castes were allowed to bring their statues of the God Ganesha in procession along with the statues belonging to higher castes in the Ganapati festival. D.K. Mohanty has argued that in 1894, an incident happened, which is worth mentioning here. When Tilak was going in a Ganapati procession, he suddenly heard a shrill cry from a widow. He saw a boy of seven to eight years crying loudly and his mother was pacifying him. On enquiry he could know from his mother that her son wanted his Ganapati to be taken to the river for immersion ceremony along with other Ganapatis but she dared not let him do that as her family belonged to the untouchable class. Tilak was moved to tears. He went into the house and brought Ganapati idol and placed it by his side. The boy also joined the procession holding on to Tilak's hand [45]. A Mahar could come and sit on his carpet at Tilak's place in Poona as easily as a higher caste man.

On 24th and 25th March, 1918, the first depressed classes conference was held in Bombay. Tilak also addressed the conference. He declared in the conference that untouchability should go. He said that because all Indians were children of the same motherland, there could be no spiritual and moral defence of untouchability. He argued, "I am for removing all caste distinctions regarding interdining or untouchability [46]. He even said, "If God were to tolerate untouchability I would not recognize him as God at all" [47]. He further argued, "This is a cancer in the body of Hindu society and we must eradicate it at all costs" [48] He added, "Let everyone aim high, muscle or the capacity for labour and bravery every Indian must develop. He must learn to live the truth that all work is noble and do away with his 'touch-me-not' notions. He must be ready to put his hands even to 'Sudra' work. And he must rouse up and foster Kshatriyatwa in himself for, in the new world every one must be a soldier on pain of national ruin. To this Sudra-Kshatriya training one may join either the Brahmin or the Vaishya education or a suitable admixture of either division. Thus equipped let every Indian place his equipment and himself at the service of the motherland [49].

It is evident from the above mentioned views that Tilak gave proper respect to all the castes. He went to the extent of saying that if God were to tolerate untouchability, he would not recognize him as God. He criticized untouchability and compared it with cancer. He said that all work was noble and for the betterment of the nation, all castes should join hands with each other.

However, Tilak was against the social reformism of Ranade, Gopal Knshan Gokhale, Bhandarkar, Byramji Malabari, Agarkar and others because they were trying to remake India almost totally in the image of the West. Lokamanya argued, "A number of our educated men began to accept uncritically the materialistic doctrines of the Westerners. Thus we have the pathetic situation of new generation making on their minds a carbon copy of the gross materialism of the West" [50]. He further said, "Our present downfall is due not to Hindu religion but to the fact that we have absolutely forsaken religion" [51]. Here, Tilak emphasized that every nation has her own circumstances and values and she should develop in her own way one should not ignore one's religion or traditions.

According to him, reform would have to be based on the value system of the people and not on the values of an alien system of education. He believed that popular education should be there. He gave importance to religion and argued, "Religious education will first and foremost engage our attention" [52] there was no need for India to copy some other civilization when she could rely on the spirit of her past greatness. D.V. Athalye argued, "The difference was this, that while Ranade was prepared, if convenient, to coquette with religious sanction to social order, Mr. Tilak insisted that there should be no divorce between the two" [53].

The Westernized social reformers were of the view that virtually everything Indian was, by definition, degraded, unprogressive and evil. Tilak was of the opinion that the cause of this was that the Westernized reformers did not understand either the classical ethics or the classical methods of meeting problems. He argued, "As the works of purely materialistic philosophers on Ethics are principally taught in our colleges the fundamental principles of the Karma-yoga, mentioned in the Gita, are not well understood even by learned persons among us who have had an English education" [54]. Tilak's cause of concern here was that those who did not know the old were preparing to construct the radically new which would destroy their civilization.

Tilak was not uprooted from his past but was rather devoted to it. Therefore, his approach was entirely different from Westernized social reformers. In his opinion, the ideas of these social reformers were based on Western value system and they had totally ignored their own ancient civilization. He argued that it was not possible to construct the new without knowing the old. According to him in that case the classical values would be lost, the moral stamina would be undermined and national will would be broken. He further said that social reforms were needed, but not in such a way as to destroy the civilization which could be reformed. To quote him, "A true nationalist desires to build on old foundations. Reform based on utter disrespect for the old does not appeal to him as constructive work. He, therefore, tries to maintain and foster a distinct national interest before undertaking any reform. We don't want to anglicize our institutions and so de-nationalise them in the name of social reform. We mean to progress and wish our country to occupy a position of equality among the civilized nations of the world. But whereas men of Mr. Paranjpye's party would ask us to adopt alien methods, even in offering our prayers to God we the nationalists desire to emphasise and preserve the national sentiment by giving due credit to all that is good in the old system but without detriment to progress and reform needed for our national uplift" [55].

Lokamanya started his fight with the atrophied spirit of orthodoxy while still engaged in his battle with the Westernized reformers. N.C. Kelkar said, "He stood midway between the immovable orthodoxy of those people who are steeped over head and ears in the traditions of olden days, and the road-hog speed of apocalyptic social revolutionists" [56]. To quote Tilak, "just as old and orthodox opinions (and their holders the Pandits, etc.) are one sided, so the new English educated reformers are also one sided and dogmatic. The old Sastries and Pandits do not know the new circumstances whereas the newly educated class of reformers are ignorant of the traditions and traditional philosophy of Hinduism. Therefore a proper knowledge of the old traditions and philosophies must be imparted to the newly educated classes, and the Pandits and Sastrles must be given information about the newly changed and changing circumstances" [57]. Tilak wanted to convey the message that the knowledge of old was a must for the new generations and it was also equally important to impart the new information to the Sastries.

According to T.L. Shay, "the degraded aspects of the spirit of orthodoxy were lethargy, indolence, exclusiveness of inaction. They had fed on disunity and divisiveness born of defensiveness and rigidity, and from this had arisen casteism in all its worst manifestations, defeatism and fatalism, the loss of the ideal of harmonious social cooperation, of courage and of self-respect in a word, the dynamics of the classical philosophy of life had been perverted into negation and passivity" [58]. This spirit, Tilak believed, was the opponent of India's progress, and it was with this spirit that he did battle. Atrophied orthodoxy had no religious justification. It seems that Tilak wanted to educate the people and make them realize that atrophied orthodoxy had no religious justification. His first task was to reach the people, for he knew that lasting change, required change in the hearts of people and not, as the reformers believed, change in the forms of institutions.

Tilak taught the Dharma of action [59]. He was of the view, "it is only man himself that can bring about his own salvation. If you don't act like human beings, of what use are you to your country?" [60] Lokamanya further argued, "No one can expect the Providence to protect one who sits with folded arms and throws his burden on others. God does not help the indolent. You must be doing all that you can to lift yourself up, and then only you may rely on the Almighty to help you" [61]. He further said that the willingness to work and sacrifice for an ideal was the prerequisite. He taught the Vedic lesson, "Whatever a man does, must be taken to have been done by him for the purpose of the 'yajna' (sacrifice) in as much as the Vedas themselves have enjoined the performance of the yajna, any Action done for the purpose of the yajna cannot of itself be a source of bondage to man" [62] Here Tilak talked about the selfless service He himself worked selflessly in the plague and Famine works etc.

Tilak disagreed with his colleagues on two fundamental issues: the time-table of change and the primacy of political change over social reform. [63] He believed that the social reformers were attempting to reconstruct society from outside with a magic wand. Co-operating with the government and the missionaries, the reformers advocated drastic measures to root out social evils, reforms which would alienate Hindu society and frustrate their purposes. However, according to Tilak only a program of gradual change based on a compromise between the reformers wishes and the society's expectations would produce lasting results.

Since the reformers could not inspire mass support for their reform programme, they sought to enforce reform through the alien state. Tilak believed that it would mean to destroy India's greatness and to use the force of an alien ruler to impose any kind of reform would be to make that reform itself immoral.

Moreover, he believed that all social evils could be mended if the country attained political freedom [64]. According to him; it was not wise to hang the problem of political emancipation and make it dependent on the attainment of social reforms. To quote him, "I don't hold that social reconstruction must be undertaken prior to political emancipation. I attach greater importance to the latter. Without the power to shape our destiny, our national regeneration in a large sense, can't in my opinion be affected that I have throughout my career tried to preach and emphasize this views" [65]. "Tilak was convinced that the emancipation of the country must have the first priority in national programme, for without it social reforms could make no real headway" [66] He gave the example of Ireland and argued that Ireland had almost concretely realized the scheme of social reforms which was suggested by the Indian social reformers but still she was politically backward.

He asserted, "There is no inherent connection or relation of cause and effect between social reform and earnestness about national regeneration. On the contrary there is a possibility of opposition between them" [67]. Tilak gave more importance to national freedom. It is a naked truth that without getting power, no nation can change her society.

Tilak resembled Aurobindo when he differed from social reformers and regarded political freedom as a prerequisite for the removal of social evils. Aurobindo argued, "The hope of social reform divorced from political freedom is an illogical hope which ignores the nature of social life and the conditions of its well-being" [68]. He said that if political freedom was denied, an individual would not be able to follow noble ends and would become a degraded person. According to him, "When man is thus degraded, it is idle to think that society can be free" [69]. Thus Aurobindo like Tilak, gave precedence to political freedom.

Lokamanya believed that there were defects in every society [70]. He said, "The social organization in India is not surely dead, it is probably slumbering and sleep is no death, and there is sure to be a waking sooner or later" [71]. He further argued that social reforms and social freedom could only be attained gradually [72]. Lokamanya hoped that Indian society would reform itself with the passage of time.

The controversy raised round the central issue whether social or political reform should come first. Tilak argued, "Swarajya alone is the root of all reforms. If you do not possess any power, you do not possess any wisdom" [73]. In this respect he differed from Agarkar who had advanced social views and had a burning passion for the eradication of the social evils. He argued that there was no harm in the foreign state making laws for social and material regulation. Tilak argued that the fundamental requirement of the country was the attainment of political freedom and not social reform. Thus, the policies with respect to social reform of Tilak and Agarkar were entirely divergent.

On this particular issue Tilak also had differences with Gokhale. Tilak and Gokhale had started a revolution in education in Maharashtra by establishing Deccan Education Society. But differences cropped up between the two. Gokhale laid much emphasis on social reforms. He believed that social reforms must be carried out to make the roads to freedom. Stanley A. Wolpert has argued that the introduction of British rule, in fact, was considered by Gokhale and his guru Ranade as the fortuitous dispensation of divine providence sent to rouse India from the lethargy of centuries, and to teach her how to remodel her institutions [74]. But Tilak argued that political freedom should precede social reforms. Once Swaraj was achieved, social reform would follow. He did not like the idea of any social reform by alien rulers. He argued, "No nation can be strong and healthy unless it is free" [75].

Tilak in his busy and eventful life concentrated on politics and went to the extent of saying that social and other reforms could be taken up latter. At any rate, in his opinion they should not be given priority [76]. He argued, "My own belief has generally been that whatever reforms we might press for would be comprised in Swarajya only" [77]. But for Gandhi, all reforms were as urgent as any other and he took them up without compartmentalizing them or fixing any priorities [78].

As against Ranade's restlessness at the prevalence of iniquitous and cruel social customs, by the side of which political subjection was insignificant, Tilak, following Chiplunkar, held that there was nothing basically wrong with their society, and it was the foreign rule which was galling. While Ranade desired that work for political and social progress should go on side by side, Tilak was impatient for political emancipation and patient regarding social reform. Tilak recognized the existence of social evils, to which reformers had pointed, and in his personal conduct he was in favour of reforms. He congratulated Bhandarkar on having married a widow. What he objected to was not social reform but a movement for social reform. According to him, political work must not only precede social reform work; the latter must be held in abeyance until political progress reached the point of national independence. According to Ranade, political progress was a matter of evolution. Tilak saw, though he did not express this in the early stages, that progress towards national freedom would require national resistance in which all people must stand united and social reform in the very nature of things would divide society into opposed groups of reformers and conservatives [79].

Tilak was of the view that the solidarity of masses in society must be preserved for the national interest. He argued, "Our main duty lies in concerting measures which will contribute to the glory of our nation. We have got to forget our differences however great they might be" [80]. While suggesting measures he said, "It is possible to unite the followers of Hinduism by the revival and growth of the Hindu 'religion', for the Hindu religion does not lie in caste, eating and drinking" [81]. He further wrote, "The word Dharma means a tie and comes from the root dhri to bear or hold. What is there to hold together? To connect the soul with God, and man with man. Dharma means our duties towards God and duty towards man. Hindu religion as such provides for a moral as well as social tie. This being our definition we must go back to the past and see how it was worked out. During Vedic times India was a self-contained country. It was united as a great nation. That unity has disappeared bringing on us great degradation and it becomes the duty of the leaders to revive that union. The gist of Dharma does not lie in rivalry, but it lies in effective union" [82]. Tilak was of the view that national interest was more important than the interests of any sects. He said, "Communal jealousies and caste rivalries are the weak points in our armour, but we must strengthen our position by sinking all differences among ourselves" [83]. He gave the message that social unity was of paramount importance. The country was not free in the times of Tilak. He wanted to awaken masses through religious education to fight for their rights. He has given broad interpretation to religion and argued that religion did not divide the people rather it united them.

According to N.C. Kelkar, "The rousing of a sense of self-respect in the Indian people, the creation of a hope of a bright future before them, the assertion of their full national rights as a nation, and the infusion of a spirit of proud and even reckless defiance of anything that may stand in the way of all this - that was the main theme of all his idealism and realism" [84]. Tilak was of the view that for the betterment of India mutual respect and unity of all the people was direly needed. In that way, through common, united efforts, social evils could be eradicated by the people.

It can be argued that Tilak was not opposed to social reforms. In fact he was a practical reformer. In the Mahrataa he argued, "We have always been advocates of reform, reform we say, but not of rebellion or licence" [85]. The reformism of Tilak was the product of his moral frame of reference, based on the Indian philosophy, and planned in accord with his own realism. He was of the view that those who believed in reform, those who were educated and posed as the leaders of the community, should be the first to practice the reforms they advocated. He further believed that the social reformers should mix with the people to educate them. The acceptance of the reforms should be democratic and moral. According to him, "There has been much talk about social reforms. But we have to bear in mind that we have to reform the masses and if we disassociate ourselves from them, reforms would become impossible. The outstanding example of this is the fact that though widow-remarriage is a desirable reform, most of the reformers cannot practice it in their families. I, therefore, think that each one should start reforms from himself and convert others through practice rather than mere theory. My main contention is that the advocates of reform should live up to their own preaching."[86] He further argued, "If the educated want to take up the social education factor, they must mix with the common people. Those who want to be the leaders of the people must be in touch with the people to understand what are their needs, how much religious ardour they have got and to what channel their energy should be turned in order to gain national good" [87]. Before Tilak preached he practiced. He was loyal both to his convictions about the need for reform and to the classical heritage. He mixed with the common people while playing his role.

He was a practical reformer who rightly believed that the reforms should be first initiated by leaders. Real change was that which came within the society and for that, proper education was direly needed. That was the democratic way. They could not force anybody to change.

Thus, it would be unjust to call Tilak as a social reactionary. There must have been some justification for misrepresentation in the fierce dust of controversy. But a deep study of Lokamanya's speeches and writings should enable us to develop an impartial assessment. It would not be fair to argue that he is against social change and social reforms.

References

1. Tilak BG. Srimad Bhagavadita-Rasasya or Karma-Yoga-Sastra, Trans. by Sukthankar, 2nd ed. (Poona: Tilak Bros), 1965, 464p.
2. Tilak BG. quoted in Pradhan GP, Bhagwat AK. Lokamanya Tilak: A Biography (Bombay: Jaico Publishing House), 1959, 56p.
3. Tilak BG. Srimad Bhagavadgita - Rahasya or Karma-Yoga-Sastra, 564-65.
4. A Step in the Steamer (Bombay: National Bureau Publishers), 1918, 76p.
5. Tilak BG. Srimad Bhagavadgita - Rahasya or Karma-Yoga-Sastra, 90p.
6. *Ibid.*, 92-93.
7. *Ibid.*, 91-92.
8. *Ibid.*, 464-65.

9. *Ibid.,* 543p.

10. *Ibid.,* 559p.

11. *Ibid.*

12. Suneera Kapoor, Sri Aurobindo Ghosh and Bal Gangadhar Tilak: The Spirit of Freedom, 47p.

13. Ravinder Kumar, ed., Selected Documents of Lokamanya Bal Gangadhar Tilok 1880, 1920; 4:61p.

14. Tilak BG. *His Writings and Speeches*, Enl. ed., (Madras: Ganesh & Co), 1919, 234p.

15. Ravinder Kumar, *op. cit.,* 62p.

16. Sri Aurobindo, the Human Cycle; the Ideal of Human Unity; War and Self-Determination (Pondicherry: Sri Aurobindo Ashram), 1977, 49p.

17. Vinod Tiwari, Bal Gangadhar Tilak, 35p.

18. Desai AR. Social Background of Indian Nationalism (Bombay: Popular Prakashan), 1948, 241p.

19. Shay TL. The Legacy of the Lokamanya: The Political Philosophy of Bal Gangadhar Tilak, 44p.

20. *Ibid.,* 56p.

21. Quoted in *Ibid.,* 62p.

22. This bill proposed to amend Section 475 of the Indian Penal Code so as to raise from ten to twelve years the age at or below which intercourse with or without consent of married or unmarried woman would constitute the offence of rape.

23. Stanley A. Wolpert, Tilak and Gokhale: Revolution and Reform in the making of Modern India, 38p.

24. Dhananjay Keer, Lokamanya Tilak: Father of the Indian Freedom Struggle, 449p.

25. *Ibid.*

26. *Ibid.*

27. Varma VP. Modern Indian Political Thought (Agra: Lakshmi Narain Agarwal), 1998, 209-10.

28. "Quoted in Mohanty DK. Indian Political Tradition: From Manu to Ambedkar, 204p.

29. *Ibid.*

30. Ram Gopal, Lokamanya Tilak: A Biography, 114p.

31. For details see Telang PK, in Bapat SV. Reminiscences and Anecdotes of Lokamanya Tilak, (Poona, S.V. Bapat). 1925; 2:27-28.

32. Kelkar NC. Full and Authentic Report of the Tilak Trial (Bombay The Indu Prakash Steam Press), 1908, 7p.

33. Shay TL. The Legacy of Lokamanya: The Political Philosophy of Bal Gangadhar Tilak, 67p.

34. Tahmankar DV. Lokamanya Tilak: Father of Indian Unrest and Maker of Modern India, 49p.

35. Jog NG. Lokamanya Bal Gangadhar Tilak, 32p.

36. Tilak BG. The Evils of Child Marriage, Mahratta. 1881; 1(22):1-8.

37. *Ibid.*

38. Samagra Lokamanya Tilak, 7: 42p.

39. Quoted in Tahmankar DV. Lokamanya Tilak: Father of Indian Unrest and Maker of Modern India, 52p.

40. *Ibid.*

41. Quoted in *Ibid.*

42. Stanley A. Wolpert, Tilak and Gokhale: Revolution and Reform in the Making of Modern India, 71p.

43. A Step in the Steamer, 32p.

44. Varma VP. The Life and Philosophy of Lokamanya Tilak, 45p.

45. Mohanty DK. Indian Political Tradition: From Manu to Ambedkar, 205p.

46. Samagra Lokamanya Tilak, 7:46p.

47. Shinde VR, in Bapat SV. Reminiscences and Anecdotes of Lokamanya Tilak, 7:204p.

48. *Ibid.*

49. Samagra Lokamanya Tilak, 7:630p.

50. Shay TL. The Legacy of the Lokamanya: The Political Philosophy of Bal Gangadhar Tilak, 64p.

51. Tilak BG. His Writings and Speeches, Enl. Ed., 3p.

52. *Ibid.,* 73p.
53. Athalye DV. The Life of Lokamanya Tilak, 54p.
54. Tilak BG. Srimad Bhagavadgita-Rahasya or Karma-Yoga-Sastra, 93p.
55. Samagra Lokmanya Tilak, 7:5p.
56. Kelkar NC. Life and Times of Lokamanya Tilak, 154p.
57. Quoted in Shay TL. The Legacy of Lokamanya: The Political Philosophy of BaI Gangadhar Tilak, 62:71-72.
58. *Ibid.,* 72p.
59. Naveen K Sharma, Lokamanya Tilak, 71p.
60. A Step in the. Steamer, 80p.
61. Tilak BG. His Writings and Speeches, 277p.
62. Tilak BG. Gita-Rahasya, 72p.
63. Richard I Cashman. The Myth of the Lokamanya Tilak and Mass Politics in Maharashtra, 53p.
64. Singh MK. ed. Encyclopaedia of Great Indian Political Thinkers, 3:22p.
65. Kelkar NC. Life and Times of Lokamanya Tilak, 42p.
66. Jyoti Sharma, Tilak and Gandhi: Perspectives on Religion and Politics, 125p.
67. Kelkar NC. Life and Times of Lokamanya Tilak, 486p.
68. Sri Aurobindo, Bande Mataram: Early Political Writings-I, (Pondicherry: Sri Aurobindo Ashram). 1972; 1:881-82.
69. *Ibid.,* 700p.
70. Samagra Lokamanya Tilak, (Poona: Kesari Prakashan). 1976; 4:774p.
71. Samagra Lokamanya Tilak. 7:548p.
72. Samagra Lokamanya Tilak, (Poona: Kesari Prakashan). 1976; 5:157p.
73. A Step in the Steamer, 157p.
74. Stanley A Wolpert. Tilak and Gokhale: Revolution and Reform in the making of modern India, 297p.
75. A Step in the Steamer, 66p.
76. Diwakar RR. "The Lokamanya and the Mahatma" in Verinder Grover, *op. cit.,* 420p.

77. A Step in the Steamer, 155p.
78. Diwakar RR. "The Lokamanya and the Mahatma" in Verinder Grover, *op. cit.,* 420p.
79. Jagirdar PJ. "Tilak and Ranade", in Verinder Grover, *op. cit.,* 533-34.
80. A Step in the Steamer, 32p.
81. Tilak BG. His Writings and Speeches, 342p.
82. *Ibid.,* 13-14.
83. *Ibid.,* 353p.
84. Quoted in Shay TL. The Legacy of Lokamanya: The Political Philosophy of Bal Gangadhar Tilak, 77p.
85. *Ibid.,* 67p.
86. Tilak BG. quoted in Pradhan GP, Bhagwat AK. Lokamanya Tilak: A Biography (Bombay: Jaico Publishing House), 1959, 52p.
87. Quoted in Shay TL. The Legacy of Lokmaṇya: The Political Philosophy of Bal Gangadhar Tilak, 69p.

Chapter - 3

Political Ideas of Tilak

It has been observed in the preceding chapter that Tilak's main concern in life was the political emancipation of India. Hence, there was an element of realism in his political ideas. But he was not a realist in the Hobbesian and Machiavellian sense of the term. His political views have not been woven into any closely knit concept or theory. Most of his ideas lie scattered here and there in his various writings and speeches. Unlike philosophers who wrote about a particular idea in a compendium, Tilak's views have emerged as reaction to a particular situation, in a particular context and on a particular issue. He was not a mere academician but primarily a political activist. Thus we do not find any systematic political philosophy in Tilak as his political activities were mainly the result of conditions and circumstances existing at that particular time.

According to Lokamanya, state was a necessary institution. He argued, "A controlling authority of some sort or other has been indispensable; and such a control cannot be exercised by a people who met together every time the need arose" [1]. He said that according to Mahabharta, a country which had no king and which had not a settled system of administration, was not fit for habitation even for a moment. There was no knowing when in such a country their lives may be lost, their wealth stolen, or their house rifled or set on fire [2]. He added, "The state of anarchy is quite different, regions beset with anarchy can never hope to rise and we are not concerned here about them" [3]. Thus, Tilak beheved that state was necessary for the survival and development of individual and society. In this respect he differed from anarchist thinkers like Aurobindo and Gandhi. In Aurobindo's ideal society there is no need of the state. To quote him, "the perfect social state must be one in which governmental compulsion is abolished and man is able to live with his fellowman by free agreement and cooperation" [4].

The ideal society conceived by Gandhi also did not leave any scope for the state. He was of the view that the ideal society was a state of enlightened anarchy in which everyone was his own ruler, and there was no political power because there was no state [5].

Tilak differed from those thinkers who talked about the organic theory of state. According to Hegel, the state was an organism, it was an end in itself. To quote him, "the state is the divine idea as it exists on earth'. For all the worth which the human being possess - all spiritual reality he possesses only through the state'. The state is the spirit which stands in the world and realizes itself there in consciously. The existence of the state is God's movement in the world.' 'The state is the divine will as the present spirit unfolding itself to the actual shape and organization of a world" [6]. The state, according to him, was the highest form of human association and beyond it, there was no higher association. But Tilak moved beyond state and talked of human unity.

Tilak resembled mechanistic thinkers of state like Aurobindo and Gandhi in rejecting the organic theory of state. He regarded the state as a means for the *welfare of* the people, and said, "We hold that welfare of the people is the real ideal and strength of the state" [7].

For Aurobindo state was nothing more than a machine. It had no soul and could not be regarded as an end. According to him, increase in the power of state posed a serious threat to individual freedom. To quote him, "The state is bound to act crudely and in the mass; it is incapable of that free, harmonious and intelligently or instinctively varied action which is proper to organic growth. For the state is not an organism; it is a machinery, and it works like a machine, without tact, taste, delicacy or intuition" [8]. He further said, "The individual has usually something at least like a soul but the state is an entity which has no soul or only a rudimentary one. It is a military; political and economic force; but it is only in a slight and undeveloped degree, if at all, an intellectual and ethical being" [9]. Gandhi also regarded the state as a soulless machine. He argued that state was not an end in itself. Similarly, Lokamanya also did not recognize state as an end.

Tilak believed in the rule of law. His notion of the state was democratic. He argued, "The public affairs have got to be carried out in accordance with the wishes of the people concerned" [10]. He believed in the idea of popular sovereignty and argued that real sovereign was the people and not the king. He said, "The king may himself be a sort of deity, but the conflict between him and his subjects begets another deity only superior to him" [11]. He further argued, "The divine king as soon as he ceases to be just ceases also to be divine. He becomes an *'asura' and* this depreciated divinity is forthwith replaced by a deity, the divinity in which is not so alloyed" [12].

Lokamanya believed that authority should be in the hands of the people. He argued, "To give authority into people's hands is the best principle of administration" [13]. He believed in a government which was for the people and not only by the people. Tilak advocated a representative government in which the wishes of the people would be respected and acted upon. In a letter to Mrs. Besant he argued that he believed in no other *Mahatnia* except the "Mahatma of Majority" [14]. Gandhi also argued that Tilak was a born democrat and believed in the rule of majority with an intensity that fairly frightened him [15]. Tilak was of the view that the extension of education and political franchise were necessary for the success of democracy" [16].

Lokamanya talked about duties of the state. However it becomes clear from his writings that he did not make a clear-cut distinction between the state and the government. To quote him, "What is then the Government for? It is for carrying out reforms that affect the welfare of the people. That is the fundamental duty of the state. I maintain that it is the primary duty of the Government to satisfy our growing aspirations. The state has no doubt built railways, put up post and telegraph offices, opened canals, and laid out roads. What I mean to say is that they ought not to remain content with doing what they have hitherto done. They should have done much more. That is my main contention" [17]. While talking about the duties of the state Tilak said that state should always try to work for the betterment of the people.

Tilak was of the view that it was the duty of Government to provide economic security to the masses. He argued, "What we maintain is that it is the duty of Government to introduce such a system of administration as would bring prosperity to the country. If Government exists, it is not merely for securing peace but for securing prosperity to the land" [18]. He further said, "If they are to be dealt with by individuals, what does the Government exist for? If we get rain every year, if there is no plague in the country, no diseases why, I am sure we can well dispense not only with Government but also with medical practitioners. The thing is that it is a clear duty of Government not to grumble at the conditions, they may be climatic or they may be economic, but to find out remedies, so that the whole of the country may enjoy prosperity, that is what the Government has to do" [19]

Tilak was in favour of the development of indigenous industry and commerce and argued that it was the duty of the Government to protect indigenous industries by imposing taxes on imports. He talked about economic rights of the people against the government. He maintained that the revenue collected by government should be used for the material improvement of the people and for the purposes of public utility. He further said that the power to decide as to how much money was to be collected, how the taxes were to be imposed and how the revenue should be spent should be in the hands of the men elected by the people.

Tilak believed that the king and the people had obligations towards each other. He gave the concept of *Prajadroha* which meant the crime of treason by the king to the people and argued that *Prajadroha* did not find place in the existing penal code. But it could find place in the penal code of God [20].

He discussed the right to resist unjust laws and said that if the law was unjust it must be resisted even at the risk of suffering the punishment. Such things were inevitable when law was divorced from morality. Thus Lokamanya was of the view that man had certain rights by nature and state could not take away those rights. He argued, "We must get the rights which belong to man by naturex" [21]. He said, "God has endowed you with free will and free power of action. If you fail to make use of it, it is not the fault of God; it is entirely yours" [22]. Hence, he wanted the people to become aware of their rights and to struggle for their attainment.

He advocated political rights of individual and believed in freedom of speech, freedom of public discussion and freedom of press. To quote him, "English Statute enacted by the Jury Act of 1792 safeguards the liberty of the English people in matters of speech, in matters of meetings, of public discussion and of public writings" [23]. He was of the opinion that Indians were also entitled to all those rights.

Tilak was of the view that people should have the right to express their views before the Government. He argued, "Administration would be impossible but for this freedom of expression. We have every right to place our views before the Government" [24]. He added, "Every man must exercise his rights over the Government, place his grievances before them and see that they are redressed. If the Government will not listen, he must compel their attention" [25]. Here Tilak wanted the people to be active about the affairs of the state.

Lokamanya also talked about the freedom of press. He argued that the press should have freedom to make the Government aware of the public opinion. He said that the mere publication of an article, whatever the context, whatever the surrounding circumstances was not an offence. To quote him, "The great error to be avoided is the error of supposing that Sedition can ever consist in the mere use of the language, abstracted from every other consideration. Such a principle would be inconsistent with the right of public discussion" [26] Tilak's views regarding the freedom of press are of the paramount importance. When he expressed these ideas, India was not free and the role of press was very crucial in awakening the mass mind.

It is observed that Tilak was influenced by *Vedantic* philosophy, Manu and Mahabharta regarding his ideas on state. He frequently referred these ancient ideas in his writings and speeches while talking about the duties of the state, he argued, "The King or sovereign is no doubt a part and parcel of the God-head, but according to the *Vedanta,* so is every member of the subject people. It is absurd to suppose that the Indian law-givers of old regarded a king absolved from all duties towards his subjects. Why Manu has distinctly laid down, for instance, that the king who punishes those whom he should not, or does not punish those whom he should, goes to hell" [27].

Lokamanya was also influenced by Western liberal ideas of the exponents of negative liberty. He wanted minimum state interference with individual liberty and opposed state interference in social and religious matters. He said, "We would certainly not like to be so ridiculed that our very customs should be regulated by the legislature. Should we not ourselves learn how to prevent the evils in our own social custom, and should we not ourselves form bodies to impose restraints on ourselves and thus leave no cause for Government interference?" [28] He added, "We do not think that any sane man would go in for Government interference in such matters. We must try to manage and regulate them ourselves." [29] He wanted a limited role of state in social and religious fields. He was of the view that it was the primary duty of the society to solve its problems and state should not interfere in it. However he was not consistent in his views regarding the role of state. On the one hand he wanted the state to bring out economic reforms and thus play a positive role but on the other hand he was opposed to the interference of the state in the social and religious matters.

Tilak attached great importance to freedom. He said, "Liberty is the birthright of every man." [30] He considered it as a natural right. He was of the view that the desire of freedom was the natural instinct in man and was "the essence of human nature." [31] He argued, "The privilege of being free is not required to be granted by somebody else" [32]. He added that the humanness of man consisted in realizing those aspirations which were bound up with the natural instinct of freedom. All other feelings must be subordinated to that one dominant sentiment, that one goal.

Lokamanya believed that freedom was a divine instinct in man and argued, "What is called *Atma* in religious philosophy is known as Liberty in the science of politics" [33]. He further held, "No weapon can cut this spirit, no fire can burn it; no water can wet it, no wind can dry it" [34]. He added, "Freedom is the very life of the individual soul, which *Vedanta* declares to be not separate from God but identical with Him. Thus, freedom was a principle that could never perish" [35]. He equated freedom with soul. According to him, soul and freedom both were immortal. While giving importance to individual freedom, he argued, "What is Good Government? It is that kind of administration under which every individual is perfectly free to develop his faculties" [36]. Tilak talked about the overall development of the individual. He regarded that government good in which every individual possessed freedom to develop his faculties.

According to Tilak, the attainment of spiritual freedom was the highest goal of man. He regarded spiritual freedom as "the fundamental pure state of the *Atman.*" [37] According to him the realization of identity of *Atman* and Brahman was the purest state *of Atman.* Talking about spiritual freedom he said, that it was a life centered in self and dependent upon itself [38]. He believed, "Whenever and wherever the complete Realization of the *Atman* comes, Release is obtained at that very moment and at that place" [39].

Like Aurobindo, Tilak subscribed to the *Vedantic* view of spiritual freedom, according to which ignorance led to bondage and spiritual knowledge led to spiritual freedom. He said, "Jnana (knowledge) is the only way to permanently escape this troublesome cycle, that is to say, to obtain release. 'Jnana' does not mean the knowledge of the ordinary things of life but the Realization of the identity of the Brahman and Atman" [40].

Tilak was of the view that for the attainment of spiritual freedom, spiritual knowledge and desireless action were required. To quote him, "It has been laid down in our religious books the *'Swara'* can be obtained only when you practice the *'Karma-yoga',* when you put forth your energies without expecting any reward in return, when you do your duty cheerfully for duty's sake, when you combine manly action with metaphysical knowledge" [41].

Tilak was of the view that one could attain spiritual freedom without renouncing the world. He argued, "I have thus solved the question for myself and I hold that serving the world; and thus serving His Will, is the surest way of salvation, and this way can be followed by remaining in the world and not going away from it" [42] He said that if we really wish to attain power in this world and also to secure the supreme spiritual bliss, we must give up false notions that induce inaction, and must apply ourselves assiduously to task of our own regeneration [43] To quote him, "Abstention from Action is not the way for escaping the bonds of Karma; that ultimate release is attained only by keeping the Mind pure, by Realizing the identity of the *Brahman* and the *Atman* and by behaving like the *Paramevvara;* and that the idea of the giving up Action is an illusion" [44]. Thus, according to Tilak it was not necessary to renounce the world for the attainment of spiritual freedom and salvation could be achieved by serving the world. He added, "It is true that obtaining Release is the duty of every man, yet, it is also essential that he should simultaneously bring about universal welfare *(Lokasamgraha)"* [45]

According to him, "there is only one *Atman* in all created beings and behaving accordingly, is the climax of spiritual knowledge" [46]. He further said, "Continually observing this Equability of Mind towards all created things in the performance of all bodily, vocal or mental Action is known as ***'nityamuktavastha'*** (state of perpetual release), ***'puma-yoga'*** (perfect yoga) or ***'siddhavastha'*** *(the* state of a perfect being)" [47].

According to Tilak there was no conflict between spiritual freedom and equality. He said, "Just as *Kubera* is never in need for a lakh of rupees, so the man whose Mind has become equable, experiences no dearth of the feeling of the identity of the Atman in the members of a family, or a country, or in co-religionists, or any other inferior order of identities. All these identities are included in the identity of the *Brahmnn* and the *Atman*" [48]. He further said, "the man, who has once accomplished this ultimate state, does not need to be taught any laws about what should be done or should not be done, i.e., of Ethics; because, as the purest the most equable and the most sinless frame of mind is the essence of morality, laying down laws of Ethics for such a *Sthttaprajna* would be as unreasonable as imaging that the Sun is surrounded by darkness, and holding up a torch for it" [49]. Tilak was of the view that there was no need to teach law and morality to a person who had attained spiritual freedom.

Lokamanya was influenced by ancient Indian ideas in his views on individual freedom and spiritual freedom. He had taken the idea of immortality of soul from *Bhagavad-Gita.* He was particularly influenced by the doctrine of *karmayoga* as expounded in Gita. Tilak was influenced by the *Vedantic* idea of the identity of soul with God. He infused new meaning to ancient Indian ideas when he equated freedom with soul. He was also influenced by the Western liberal notion of rights. To quote him, "Why should we be afraid of the liberal thoughts of free Englishman? Do not suppose that the Western Countries have no *Vedantins,* and that the *Vedantins* are confined only to this country. But the Western *Vedantins* hold that the people who wield no political power are a race of dehumanized human beings" [50]. Tilak recognized that ancient Indian philosophy was mainly concerned with the spiritual freedom. It did not give due attention to social and political freedom. To quote him, "our religious literature seems to be devoted almost exclusively to the attainment of the spiritual kingdom" [51]

However, Tilak also gave importance to external freedom. He said, "How strange it is that our people who are so busy with trying to achieve bliss in the other world, should hold themselves aloof from the present struggle of our liberation" [52]. He added, "What is called 'Swarajya' or the spiritual bliss is not at all different from the 'Swarajya' or the people's government or kingdom for which we are all striving today. Our aim ought not to be the attainment of only one of these kingdoms, we must secure both" [53].

According to him, spiritual freedom could not be achieved without political freedom. Thus he said, "it is my thesis, that *Swaraj* in the life to come cannot be the reward of a people who have not enjoyed it in this world" [54].

Lokamanya interpreted the Vedantic idea of spiritual freedom in terms of national freedom. He argued that according to *Vedanta* man had the potentiality to become God himself and raised the question that if that was true, could the Indians not attain self-government?

He added that there was no conflict between *Vedantic* ideals and patriotic ideals. He was of the opinion that spiritual freedom was not at all different from people's government and argued that their religious books guided them that spiritual freedom could be realized by the desireless performance of their duty, Tilak believed that if that was true in the case of an individual, it must be true in the case of a nation also. Thus according to him, national freedom could also be realized by performing duty with a desireless frame of mind.

Lokamanya was influenced by Western liberal ideas in his views on external freedom. Like the German idealists, he conceived of freedom as the essence of spirit. He did not view liberty as the freedom to do what one desired, and regarded the transcendence of ego, as a precondition for the attainment of freedom. In this regard he resembled the exponents of positive freedom. However unlike Hegel and Bosanquet, he did not have an exalted conception of the state. He regarded self-discipline necessary for the realization of freedom and did not stress the reliability of freedom only in and through the state. Thus it can be argued that Tilak's ideas on freedom were based on a fusion of the ideas of Western liberal tradition with the ideas of ancient Indian thought.

He put forward a positive political programme which centered around the concept of *swaraj* for India. *Swaraj* is a positive concept implying self-subjection, self-realisation, self-rule or self-regulation. He started preaching the need of *swaraj* as early as 1885. Tilak borrowed the term *swaraj* from the Vedic term *'swarajyam'*.

Because of his spiritual approach, Tilak regarded *swarajya* not only a right but a *Dharma.* Politically, *swarajya* meant Home Rule or self-rule. He also gave a moral and spiritual meaning of *swarajya.* Morally, it meant the attainment of the perfection of self-control which was essential for performing one's duty. It also meant spiritual inner freedom and contemplative delight. Talking about Swaraj Tilak said, "It is a life centered in self and dependent upon self. There is *swaraj* in this world as well as in the world here after. The rishis who laid down the law of duty betook themselves to forests, because the people were already enjoying *swarajya* or people's dominion which was administered and defended in the first instance by the *kshtriya* kings. It is my conviction it is my thesis that *swaraj* in the life to come cannot be the reward of a people who have not enjoyed it in this world" [55] Hence he wanted both political liberty and spiritual freedom.

In the political sense, Lokamanya recognized four connotations of the term *swaraj.* Firstly, it meant that the ruler and the ruled should be of the same country, same religion or race. Secondly, it referred to a well governed state or system of rule of law. Thirdly, it meant a government promoting the well-being of the masses. Fourthly, it meant a government elected by and responsible to the people. He supported the right of the people to participate in the government of their country [56].

Tilak was of the opinion that the greatest evil of the day was the British *Raj.* It was immoral and therefore it had to be done away with. This led Tilak to demand *Swaraj* in the sense of self-government. It was in the course of Tilak's political activities during 1895-97 that he gave to the emerging extremist group its goal, viz., *swaraj* or self-government and the slogan: *'Swaraj* is my birth right and I will have It' [57].

Tilak was also inspired by Western liberal ideas in his views on self-government. Quoting John Stuart Mill he said, "according to Mill 'No Nation has a moral right to keep another nation in slavery such an ungodly attempt cannot be justified morally. The nation that strives to uphold slavery will have to answer for its conduct before the Highest Tribunal of the Almighty" [58].

The Britishers denied political freedom to India on the contention that the Indians were not fit for the same. Tilak tried to refute that argument and argued that Indians were capable and fit for running their public affairs. They could run the administration of their country properly. He raised the question - "Why are we not fit? Have we not eyes? Have we not ears? Have we no intelligence? Can we not write? Can we not read books? Are we incapable for riding? Why should we be unfit? You say we have not done our work; but we reply, why did you not assign any task to us? How could we do our work when it was not at all entrusted to us? Can it bc said that you had given us some work and we have failed to do that? Then how can you say that we are unfit" [59].

Tilak was of the view that Indians were never in the state of anarchy and Britishers had no right to govern Indian people. To quote him, "no civilized nation should be governed by any other nation without its consent" [60].

Tilak devoted his entire life to promote the cause of national freedom. According to him, the greatest impediment in the way of development of Indian nation was the foreign rule. The last words which he uttered on his death-bed pertain to national freedom. He argued, "Unless *Swaraj* is achieved, India shall not prosper; it is required for our very existence" [61]. Therefore, the first task before him was to throw off the yoke of the foreign regime. He said, "Man's distinction from the beasts consists in seeing whether there is any scope for the free development of his faculties, for his capacities, for his enterprise. India does not as yet afford such a free scope in these directions" [62]. He further said, "Until the administration is made responsible to the people, however strenuously and in whatever direction we may exert ourselves, we are bound to meet with discomfiture, and our ideal is bound to remain unrealized. As long as the nation is not free to accomplish its own good and has not in its own hands the power to carry out the wishes of the people, so long our inferiority and helplessness cannot cease" [63].

Tilak argued that *Swaraj* was the pre-condition for the very existence of the nation. He believed that all progress, all hope for national advancement, rested on *swaraj.* Thus, he said, "No nation can be strong and healthy unless it is free" [64]. He further argued, "Indeed, there can be no real progress without liberty. All capacity for initiative is paralysed. Self-confidence is undermined. In countless invisible ways subjection demoralizes nations and retards both their moral and material progress" [65]. Tilak was of the view that the people could not attain economic freedom under the alien rule. He said that economic freedom could be achieved after the attainment of political freedom. He argued, "Several eminent thinkers have devoted their attention to the question of the economic regeneration of India, and if I were to sum up the result of their investigations, I would say that India could not attain greatness, unless she was in possession of the elementary rights of self-government" [66]. Thus, Tilak differed from moderate leaders who regarded the foreign rule as a divine dispensation.

Moreover, he demanded freedom of India for the purpose of ensuring peace in the world. According to him, a free India could strive to become a leading power in Asia if not in the world. Thus, he argued, "it is, therefore, absolutely necessary that India should be self-governed internally, and be made the bulwark of liberty in the East" [67].

Tilak was one of the earlier exponents of the philosophy and action programme of Indian nationalism during British occupation. Aurobindo Ghosh emphasized the spiritual aspect of Indian nationalism. But Tilak's conception of Indian nationalism was an amalgam of diverse strands of thought: pride in the legacy of ancient India; appreciation of the role of British rule in bringing about the political and administrative unification of the country; appreciation of western learning and science; recognition of economic exploitation by foreign rulers; and the recognition of the need to form a national political movement of the people across the barriers of race, caste, religion and sex [68]. These elements were fused together to make up Tilak's concept of nationalism.

Tilak asserted that since Indian civilization was most ancient and coupled with wisdom, Indian people did not have to look for any countries like England for the ways and means of socio-politico-economic programme of reconstruction. Stanley A. Wolpert said, "In a land where antiquity was generally equated with superiority, few contributions to the inflation of the national ego were of greater significance than Tilak's attempt to prove that his Aryan forebears had not merely been among the first people to attain a high level of civilization, but actually planted the seed of civilized existence in the world" [69].

Tilak appreciated the role of British rule in bringing about the political and administrative unification of the country. He was of the opinion that Britishers had given modern laws, administrative techniques and political tactics. They developed means of communication and transportation in India for their own benefit but it helped to unite Indian nation. The English language played an important role as 'Lingua Franca' in India. Indian people were also influenced by Western learning and science. They came to know the modern Western concepts of Liberty, Equality, Justice and Democracy. Through all these factors Indian masses became aware about their rights and duties. It inspired them to fight for the cause of national emancipation. Jayashree B. Gokhale has argued that the three phases of the Indian responses to the British presence in India were revival, reform and revolution" [70].

Tilak's nationalism has economic foundation also. He argued that

British Government was using India as its biggest market and destroying Indian Industries. He shared the economic views of the moderates like Ranade, Naoroji, R.C. Dutt and Gokhale. But unlike them, he maintained that economic issues had to be exploited to rouse the people's political consciousness and strengthen the freedom struggle. He did not have sufficient spare time to develop economic thought. However, he did write in *Kesari* on land revenue and land tenure systems, agricultural development, money lending and cooperative societies, need of industrialization and protection to arts and crafts, oppressive tax system and wasteful government expenditure on wars and pomp and vanity of the officials.

Lokamanya endorsed in his writing the 'drain theory' propounded by Dadabhai Naoroji. He shared Ranade's concern for industrialization of the nation. But he expressed serious difference with Ranade on the latter's defence of the British rule in regard for its role in investment in industrial, transport and communications development, growth of external and internal trade and ancillary services etc. Tilak also shared R.C. Dutt's anxiety over the deteriorating rural situation evident in recurring famines and the growing indebtedness of the farmers. But while Dutt was a moderate in his political outlook, Tilak was an extremist. He strove to mobilise the peasants, artisans, craftsmen and urban dwellers into the freedom struggle.

Tilak played a very significant role in mobilizing the masses and in giving a new turn to nationalism. Describing the condition of India before the emergence of Tilak on Indian political scene, D.V. Athalye said that, "a vast country governed recklessly, despotically and unsympathetically by a handful of foreigners, with the children of the soil most inert, the educated class timid, weak and vacillating, such was the India which young Tilak saw" [71].

Tilak seemed to be aware of the fact that national freedom would prove to be an illusion unless political and national consciousness of the people was aroused and awakened and developed strategies for the development of national consciousness of the Indians.

Lokamanya believed that the sentiment of nationalism, to be real and durable must be founded on longstanding historical and cultural modes and personalities. He had confidence that traditional culture had the power to guide the present. Thus, towards the end of the nineteenth and beginning of twentieth century he started Ganapati Festival and Shivaji Festival to boost up the morale of Maratha Nation and bring the Hindu masses on one platform through arranging these two festivals to move in the congregation.

As a mark of his technique of mass awakening, he revived some of the old practices of Hindu religion. He therefore, introduced Ganesh Festival, a Hindu God, as a public function in Maharashtra in 1893 with two objectives. Firstly, to revive the nationalist spirit and secondly, to bring oneness among the people.

Tilak not only took a prominent part in organizing the Ganapati festival in Poona but also did his best to popularize it all over Maharashtra by public lectures and articles in the *Kesar..* He referred to the Olympic festival of ancient Greece and to similar festivals of other countries and exhorted the public to participate wholeheartedly in the Ganapati festival which, from the very beginning, was observed without distinction of caste. This festival appealed so instinctly to the hearts of the people that it spread rapidly beyond Poona from place to place. Even in the year 1896, it had become a national festival. Thus, Tilak succeeded in his mission to awaken the masses for the national cause.

Tilak's ingenuity in harnessing every movement for the national cause was also illustrated by the Shivaji festival. He discovered the great potentialities of the idea of the Shivaji festival, developed it through the *Kesari* and with the help of outside propaganda gave it almost a lasting shape. The festival which became an important feature in the calendar of modern political movements not only in Poona but in the other parts of India, was a positive proof of the foresight of the original founder.

Tilak introduced Shivaji festival to remind the people about the heroic deeds of Shivaji. He tried to generate a feeling among the masses that they belonged to Shivaji's country. He also tried to teach Indians to shun western influences and feel proud of their glorious past. The Shivaji festival was inaugurated in 1896. If Ganapati was a mythological character, Shivaji, the founder of the Maratha Empire, was a historic figure. How closely Maharashtian sentiment was bound up with Shivaji was highlighted when even the British rulers utilized his name in aid of recruitment in Maharashtra in the two World Wars. Tilak wanted to awaken and unite the people against British rule through these festivals. Because his main aim was the freedom of the country and it was the need of the hour.

Another factor which helped in mobilizing the masses was Tilak's speeches. His speeches full of vigour and enthusiasm at public places, meetings and festivals made a direct impact upon the masses. Through his speeches Tilak made the people realize oppressive policies of the Government and that they had the power to resist and overthrow the Government and the importance of the political independence. Highlighting the significance of Tilak's speeches, Bapat has argued that apart from his style, his real power consisted in the way in which he accurately interpreted the mass mind. Tilak seemed to say in appropriate words exactly what each one felt. This really was the secret of his influence with the people.

Lokamanya's life was full of dynamic activities. For serving the nation on broader scale he dedicated himself to journalism. He used his writings in journals to awaken the masses for the cause of national emancipation. The two journals *Kesari* and *Mahratta* established by him and his co-patriots served him with a media to mobilize the masses on political issues and to raise their political consciousness.

Through his *Gita Rahasya* he gave a great message to the masses and infused in them the spirit of action. His work stressed the doctrine of *Karma-yoga* insisting upon the warrior's duty to fight. And through this doctrine Tilak sought to stir the Indian masses to resistive action against the alien Government. Through all these means he infused in masses the love for their nation and culture. He instilled in them the spirit of action, sacrifice and self-help and resistance against the foreign regime.

Tilak's contribution also lies in devising the basic techniques of struggle against foreign regime. He differed from the moderates regarding the methods for the achievement of *swaraj.* According to him, it was not possible to realize *swaraj* by prayers and petitions. He said, "We are against the policy of mendicancy; for it has been found, this policy would not yield the fruit but would demoralize us" [72]. His methods were based on his emotional bond and self-pride of being an Indian, his intense urge to make the Indians self-governing and at the same time his political insight to study the reality.

In this respect, Tilak differed from his contemporary, Gokhale. In politics Gokhale was a moderate but Tilak was an Extremist. Gokhale wanted to spiritualise politics. But on the other hand Tilak was of the view that politics was a game of worldly people. Gokhale believed in persuasion, appeal and protest but Tilak sought to inculcate self-respect, self-reliance and strength. Tilak was aggressive and he believed in mass action. On the other hand Gokhale believed in moderate way.

Tilak asserted that for the attainment *of swaraj* courage, suffering and sacrifice were direly needed. He stressed on self-help to realize *swaraj* and argued that God helped those who helped themselves. That truth was discovered long ago and appeared in *Rig Veda.* According to him, *swarajya* was not a fruit ready at once to fall into the mouth from the sky. Nor was another man competent to put it into their mouth. It could only be achieved by hard-work. Tilak inspired the masses to strive for the attainment of that goal unitedly. He called upon the people to sacrifice their very best for the attainment *of swaraj.* To quote him, "I preach fixed determination to reach the goal at any sacrifice" [73]. He further said, "How can light be seen unless you pass through darkness? Says an English proverb. The Sun himself has to wade his way through darkness before he brings you the morning. There is no other way to attain liberty unless you pass through the brow-beating of bureaucrats" [74].

Tilak taught people to watch the administration of the day with vigilance and trained them up in organized opposition against the foreign rule. He showed by personal example how to suffer for one's convictions and one's country. Thus, he placed a definite goal of *swaraj* before the masses and called them to devote their whole energies towards the attainment of that goal.

On January 2, 1907, in his celebrated speech on 'Tenents of the New Party', he said, "The point is to have the entire control in our hands. I want to have the key of my house, and not merely one stranger turned out of it. Self-government is our goal; we want a control over our administrative machinery. We do not want to become clerks. At present we are clerks and willing instruments of our own oppression in the hands of an alien government" [75].

Lokamanya argued that the British rule over India was based on cooperation of Indian masses. He suggested the Indian people to withdraw their support. Thinkers like Thoreau and Tolstoy had developed the idea of passive resistance. Tilak and Aurobindo advised the masses to put it into practice. Later on, this idea was practiced by Gandhi in his own way.

In a speech at Poona in 1902 he said, "You must realize that you are a great factor in the power with which administration in India is conducted. You are yourselves the useful lubricants which enable the gigantic machinery to work so smoothly. Though down-trodden and neglected, you must be conscious of your power of making the administration impossible if you but choose to make it so" [76].

It is observed that Tilak thought about passive resistance programme with different objectives. He wanted to destroy the hypnotic spell, which had made the people accept the omnipotence of their rulers. He also tried to create in the people a passionate love of liberty with a spirit of sacrifice and sufferings for the cause of the nation. He, along with Aurobindo, led the passive resistance programme of boycott, *swadeshi* and national education.

Boycott was a technique to fight against the foreign regime by refusing to co-operate with that regime. Tilak wrote articles about boycott and argued that a boycott on a national scale was the proper remedy, but its result depended upon their actions and not upon words.

Lokamanya used boycott in economic, political, nationalistic and democratic fields. He opposed the decision when excise duty on Indian cloth was raised in order to balance the custom duty imposed on British cloth. He appealed the Indian masses to boycott foreign cloth and use *swadeshi* cloth. According to Tilak, the war was not the alternative. The best alternative was to refuse to buy the British goods and not to co-operate with the Government in any sphere.

He argued, "It appears that many people have not grasped the full significance of the boycott movement. Such measures are absolutely necessary especially when there is struggle going on between a people and their alien rulers. We have neither the power nor the inclination to take up arms against the Government. But should we not try to stop the drain of millions of rupees from the country? Do we not see how the Chinese boycott of American goods has opened the eyes of the United States Government? History abundantly proves that a subject people, however helpless, can by means of unity, courage and determination overcome their haughty rulers without resort to arms. We, therefore, feel confident that people in other parts of the country will not fail to lend a helping hand to the Bengalis in the present crisis" [77].

It seems that he adopted this technique of boycott during India's freedom struggle for certain reasons. Firstly, to carry out the *swadeshi* movement. Secondly, to protest against the bad laws and taxes on the people. Thirdly, to serve as a substitute for war and violent methods which Tilak thought, would not have been possible against British rule. Gradually, the idea of boycott became an All-India political weapon. It was the first principle of the programme of Tilak and other nationalist leaders. In fact, boycott foreshadowed non-cooperation.

Swadeshi was another technique of passive resistance. It meant the use of indigenous goods and to give up the use of foreign goods. The aim of *Swadeshi* was to end the economic exploitation and to get economic and ultimately political freedom.

It is observed that Tilak had given a call to start *swadeshi* movement in India long before Gandhi. *Swadeshi,* with its implication of boycott of British goods, had been suggested as early as 1881 in Maharashtra. During Bengal partition, Tilak argued that *swadeshi* and *swadeshi* alone should be their cry for ever. He used the term *swadeshi* in dual sense, i.e., economic and political. He realized that Britishers had destroyed India's economy. He suggested the masses to prefer Indian goods. Where Indian goods were not available, they should be ready for sacrifice. Lokamanya became the real *swadeshi* in his personal life. He used the *swadeshi* paper for his journals. When *swadeshi* paper was not available, he used non-British paper. He advised the people to start cottage industries and support the 'Paisa Fund' movement, which was started in 1903. The purpose of the 'Paisa Fund' was to encourage Indian industries. He took initiative to establish the Bombay *swadeshi* cooperative stores. During the anti-partition agitation in Bengal, he inaugurated *swadeshi* exhibitions in Calcutta.

According to Dhanahjay Keer, Tilak emphasized the point that unless the people began to use articles manufactured in their country there would be no encouragement to their own producers. It was foolish to wait till all articles were available in the country. The rulers had two prominent traits in them, the trader and the politician. If the one was pressed, he concluded, the other was bound to be affected.

He also used *swadeshi* as a political weapon. Tilak argued that the people should restore faith in their culture, civilization and economic system. It would help them to take control of their political system. Referring to the *swadeshi* as an economic-cum-political weapon, he said, "If we do not wish to be white men's slaves, we should vigorously carry on the *swadeshi* movement. It is the only effective method for our deliverance. The object of the movement is to do away with the system under which we are treated like slaves by Europeans and to force Government to give us all the rights of British citizenship" [78].

Lokamanya gave a broader meaning to *swadeshi,* which was in the beginning a form of economic boycott only. He said that the object of *swadeshi* was to bring about the spread of country made goods, visible and invisible, to bring about the gradual disappearance of visible foreign things, and to bring about the gradual disappearance of foreign ideas and ideals also. According to him, the minds and bodies should also become *swadeshi.*

These ideas of boycott and *swadeshi* advocated by Tilak and Aurobindo were latter on developed by Gandhi into a potent weapon to strike the roots of British rule in India. These very ideas formed the basis of Gandhi's Non-Co-operation Movement of 1920-22 and the Civil Disobedience Movement of 1930-32.

Tilak also emphasized the role of education in the liberation of the country. He was of the view that it would make the people aware and make them understand the message of national liberation. Hence, he devoted the early years of his public life in spreading education. No doubt, Tilak recognized the role of Western education in bringing about awakening in the educated Indians by stressing the values of freedom, rights and democracy.

But at the same time, he argued that it would sow the seeds of its own destruction in India. Tilak envisaged a system of national education, which would develop the nationalist character. He was of the view that national education was direly needed to achieve the goal of *swaraj*. During 1907-08 he delivered a series of special lectures on national education in different places of Maharashtra [79].

He was actively associated with the programme of national education. He was of the view that Western education was dangerous to the future and welfare of the country. He argued that such education was keeping away the Indian people from the value system of India's civilization. He advocated the establishment of national schools and colleges throughout the country to provide inexpensive and wholesome education envisaging the new spirit of self-help and self-dependence. He argued that they must have education on national lines, and for that there must be schools fully under the control of national leaders. In the absence of such institutions, all Government or semi-Government schools, were mere mockeries [80]. According to him a nation, that had not taken its education in its own hands, could not rise in literary, social or political importance [81].

As far as the question of means for the attainment of national freedom were concerned, it is observed that Tilak was of the view that the people should use legitimate means for the attainment of *swaraj*. He argued, "I do not preach unruliness or illegality" [82]. However, he said that the agitation of the people against foreign rule should be guided by justice and morality. Therefore, he suggested that the people should not obey such laws which were opposed to justice and morality. Thus, Tilak said, "So long a lawmaking is not in our hands, laws which are repugnant to justice and morality would be sometimes passed. We cannot obey them. Passive resistance is the means to an end but is not the goal in itself. Passive resistance meant that we have to balance the advantages and disadvantages arising from obeying a particular order and not obeying it. If in our balanced judgement, we found that the advantages of disobeying it under particular circumstances were greater, the sense of morality will justify them in acting upon that conviction" [83].

During the passive resistance of 1905 to 1908 against the partition of Bengal, he condemned colonial laws as unjust and oppressive. Like T.H. Green, he justified direct political action against bad laws. Tilak not only theorized about the right to resist bad laws but also practiced it.

However, he was not consistent regarding the means to be employed for the attainment of *swaraj*. He said that the struggle for national emancipation was to be legal, but then he said that those laws which were opposed to justice and morality could not be obeyed.

There are different opinions about Tilak among the scholars about his being an advocate of violence and revolution. Chirol argued that Tilak had been the first to create the atmosphere which bred murders. John S. Hoyland the biographer of Gokhale asserted that Tilak had been coquetting with doctrines of physical force. Branson the advocate-general who conducted the prosecution case against Tilak in 1908 said that Tilak's articles contained a covert threat of mutiny and in substance he was preaching *swarajya* or bombs [84].

It is observed that Lokamanya never advocated the absolute form of non-violence as upheld by the pacifists and Tolstoy. He supported the action of Shivaji in killing Afzal Khan. He appreciated the bravery and skill of Chapekar and patriotic fervour of the Bengal revolutionaries. He adopted from *Gita* the virtue of performance of one's duty. He was of the view that the duty was supreme, and in course of discharging it without any selfish motive, if one had to do some unpleasant things, one should not hesitate on the score. True non-violence was an eternal moral ideal, but in actual practice it was very difficult to stick to it under all situations. He put the highest premium on the purification of intentions as a moralist. He argued that the external action could never be regarded as the yardstick of moral worth. Hence, if an Arjuna or a Shivaji or any other patriot would commit some violent deed, being impelled by higher altruistic motives, Tilak would not condemn such persons. But he never preached political murder nor did he ever provoke anyone to commit murder as a political means.

Moreover, Tilak did not believe in the efficacy of violent actions. He said, "I have no hesitation in saying that the acts of violence which have been committed in the different parts of India are not only repugnant to me, but have, in my opinion, only unfortunately retarded, to a great extent, the pace of our political progress. Whether looked at from an individual or from a public point of view, they deserve, as I have said before on several occasions, to be equally condemned" [85].

Aurobindo moved a step further and justified every means, including violence, for the realization *of swaraj.* He argued, “Liberty is the life-breath of a nation; and when the life is attacked, when it is sought to suppress all chance of breathing by violent pressure, any and every means of self preservation becomes right and justifiable” [86]. He added, “The *Gita* is the best answer to those who shrink from battle as a sin, and aggression as a lowering of morality” [87]. He justified the use of violence in Russia and Ireland where liberty was denied.

On the other hand, Gandhi totally ruled out violence under all circumstances. He believed that violence could not be justified even for the achievement of good ends. He was of the view that the *Gita* “has not established the necessity of a physical warfare; on the contrary, has proved its futility” [88]. Because, even after winning the battle Pandavas decided to renounce the world out of frustration. He said that selflessness taught by *Gita* was incompatible with violence. Thus, the whole idea of Gandhi’s nationalism revolved around his idea of non-violence. To quote him, “it is my dream that my country may win its freedom through non-violence. And, I would like to repeat to the world times without number, that I will not purchase my country’s freedom at the cost of non-violence” [89].

Tilak personally did not advocate either petitioning or violent methods for the attainment of *swaraj.* Being a realist, he argued that different people had different temperaments and said that every individual should contribute for the attainment of *swaraj* in his own way and choose anything from begging to open rebellion according to his ability and capacity and do it. To quote him, “Let each patriot do what he deems best for his country. Let not others put obstacles in his way. There is room in our country for different kinds of men and for different kinds of activities. One need not clash with the other. Let all acts of construction go on, whatever they and their forms may be. Let no one be disheartened by his failures or suffering in the course of his work to attain *swaraj.* Failures will bring knowledge and success” [90].

Tilak has been accused that his nationalism had a revivalist orientation and for being anti-Muslim in his approach. It is argued that he wanted to bring to the front the message of the *Vedas* and the *Gita* for providing spiritual energy and moral enthusiasm to the nation which alienated the Muslims from the nationalist movement spearheaded by him.

Palme Dutt has argued that in the first great wave of national awakening in the pre-war years, the leaders of the militant national movement, Tilak, Aurobindo Ghose and others, sought to build their agitation on a basis of

Hindu religion and tried to identify the national awakening with a revival of Hinduism. By this act they cut off the Moslem masses from the national movement, and opened the way to the government's astute counter-move with the formation of the Moslem League in 1906.

Tilak was criticized for having a communal approach in organising the Ganapati and Shivaji festivals. It is true that he had ideas of strong Hindu solidarity when he started the Ganapati festival. Kelkar has argued that Tilak himself admitted that the arrogance of the Muslim gave rise to the idea of the festival which was obviously intended to draw all the Hindus around a central national function. Tilak often justified it by saying that there was nothing wrong in providing a platform for all the Hindus of all high and low classes to stand together and discharge a joint national unity [91]. Thus, it is clear that the Ganapati festival was at best a defensive institution. It was not anti-Muslim but Hindu solidarity was its guiding principle.

V.P. Varma has argued that the police reports of Government of Bombay tried to pervert the nature of Ganapati festival. The Report of the Rowlatt Committee tried to give a highly anti-Muslim character to the Ganapati festival [92]. So greatly prejudiced was their starting-point that they have never cared to differentiate between anti-Moslemism and Hindu solidarity [93].

Zacharias has argued that Tilak was the spokesman of an anti-Muslim retaliation. A British historian Powell Price was of the view that the Muslim League which was an answer to the Indian National Congress became necessary because the possibility of self-government raised the spirit of separation which the intolerance of Tilak had emphasized [94].

Chirol was of the view that due to Tilak's extreme orthodoxy the Muslim member's of the Poona Sarvajanik Sabha resigned from that body. But all these are partial and even incorrect interpretations of the political thought and action of Tilak. Jinnah, Dr. M.A. Ansari and Hasan Imam have eloquently testified to the nationalistic sentiments and spirit of compromise of Tilak, because due to his wise counsel and moderation the Lucknow Part could be agreed upon. Shaukat Ali and Hasarat Mohani regarded Tilak as their political *Guru.* Shaukat Ali said, "I would like to mention again for the hundredth times that both Mohammed Ali and myself belonged and still belong to Lokamanya Tilak's political party" [95]. Hasarat Mohani argued, "I, even at that early age, chose the Lokamanya as the ideal leader for me. During that period I had ample opportunities of appreciating the thought and ability of almost all Indian Political leaders and basing my remarks on that close personal study, I can state without the least fear of contradiction, that I found the Lokamanya greater and superior to every other leader in every respect. When I declare that all through Tilak's life I was both intellectually and practically a blind follower of his, anyone can well judge thereby, of that love that I cherished towards him" [96]. Hasan Imam as the President of the Bombay Special Congress went to the extent of saying Tilak was his father in Indian politics. He argued, "Let me say, and it is with great pride, that Lokamanya Tilak is my father in point of politics" [97]. Furthermore, Tilak had promised to support the Khilafat movement if the majority of the Muslims were behind that. Tilak proposed the Congress resolution for the release of the Ali brothers. If Tilak would have been anti-Muslim he could never had commanded the confidence of these great Muslim leaders. Hence, it can be said that with the profoundest regard for Hinduism in private life, as a political leader, Tilak had a broad policy calculated to lead to national emancipation.

Moreover, Tilak's nationalism never suffered from narrow chauvinism or aggressiveness. According to him, love of the country was only a step to cosmopolitanism. He believed that the whole world was one big family. Though he gave importance to nation, he did not consider nation as the highest synthesis. To quote him, "that real spirit is to make the country four family instead of working only for your own. The step beyond it is to serve humanity and the next step is to serve God" [98].

Thus, Lokamanya went beyond nation and talked about humanity. He argued, "If the Vedantic ideal is higher, it necessarily included the national ideal which is the lower. There is no conflict between Vedantic ideals and patriotic ideals. One includes the other much in the same way as a thousand includes five hundred. The two ideals are mutually consistent and both of them demand a kind of self-control. Both of them demand in addition to self-control and self-sacrifice, a kind of higher altruistic feeling by which man is impelled to ignore selfish consideration and to work for persons and for objects which do not in the least savour of any egoistic aim. The feeling is one of love for humanity, for the quality of man before God, and it is the spirit of that feeling that governs the two ideals, Vedantic and national" [99]. Here, Tilak talked about human unity. For that purpose, he suggested that there should be self-control, self-sacrifice, a kind of higher altruistic feeling which ignored selfish consideration. It demanded work for humanity. He argued that *Vedaniic* ideal and national ideal were not opposed to each other.

Similarly, Aurobindo argued, "In India we do not recognize the nation as the highest synthesis to which we can rise. There is a higher synthesis, humanity, beyond that there is a still higher synthesis, this living, suffering, aspiring world of creatures, the synthesis of Budhism; there is a highest of all, the synthesis of God, and that is the Hindu synthesis, the synthesis of Vedanta" [100].

The idea of human unity expressed by Tilak and Aurobindo was further developed by Gandhi. His nationalism can best be described as Internationalists' **nationalism. To quote him,** "Just as the cult of patriotism teaches us today that the individual has to die for the village, the village for the district, the district for the province, and the province for the country, even so, a country has to be free in order that it may die, if necessary, for the benefit of the world" [101].

It is evident from the preceding discussion that Tilak was an Indian statesman with a cosmopolitan outlook who formulated his own conceptions of national interest and national progress and made his assessments of elements which helped or hindered the achievement of each. Upon these formulations and assessments he based his line of action. He played a key role in the history of Indian nationalism.

References

1. A Step in the Steamer, 101p.
2. *Ibid.,* 100p.
3. *Ibid.*
4. Sri Aurobindo, the Human Cycle; the Ideal of Human Unity; War and Self Determination (Pondicherry: Sri Aurobindo Ashram), 1971, 204p.
5. Gandhi MK. Democracy: Real and Deceptive (Ahmedabad: Navajivan Publishing House), 1961, 28p.
6. Hobhouse LT. Metaphysical Theory of the State (London: Allen and Unwin), 1926, 20p.
7. Tilak BG. quoted in Pradhan GP, Bhagwat AK. Lokamanya Tilak: A Biography, 34p.
8. Quoted in Suneera Kapoor, Sri Aurobindo Ghosh and Bal Gangadhar Tilak: The. Spirit of Freedom, 50p.
9. *Ibid.*
10. A Step in the Steamer, 62p.
11. Tilak BG. His Writings and Speeches, 75p.

12. *Ibid.,* 76p.

13. *Ibid.,* 119p.

14. All about Lokamanya Tilak (Madras: Ramaswamy Sastrulu & Sons), 1922, 130p.

15. *Ibid.*, 362p.

16. Samagra Lokamanya Tilak. 7:296p.

17. A Step in the Steamer, 63-64.

18. Sarnagra Lokamanya Tilak. 7:424p.

19. *Ibid.*

20. Samagra Lokamanya Tilak, (Poona: Kesari Prakashan). 1976; 5:157p.

21. Tilak BG. His Writings and Speeches, 164-65.

22. A Step in the Steamer, 76p.

23. *Ibid.,* 85p.

24. A Step in the Steamer, 99p.

25. Tilak BG. His Writings and Speeches, 337p.

26. Sarnagra Lokamanya Tilak, 7:60p.

27. Tilak BG. His Writings and Speeches, 74-76.

28. Tilak BG. The Evils of Child Marriage, Mahratta. 1881; 1(32):1-8.

29. *Ibid*

30. A Step in the Steamer, 39p.

31. *Ibid.,* 185p.

32. *Ibid.,* 39-40.

33. *Ibid.,* 40-41.

34. Tilak BG. His Writings and Speeches, 241p.

35. *Ibid.,* 307p.

36. A Step in the Steamer, 74p.

37. Tilak BG. Srimad Bhagavadgita-Rahasya or Karma-Yoga-Sastra, 343p.

38. Tilak BG. His Writings and Speeches, 245p.

39. Tilak BG. Sriniad Bhagauodgita-Rahasya or Karma-Yoga-Sastra, 343p.

40. *Ibid.,* 380-81.

41. A Step in the Steamer, 71p.

42. Tilak BG. His Writings and Speeches, 234-35.

43. A Step in the Steamer, 73p.

44. Tilak BG. Srimad Bhagavadgita-Rahasya or Karma-Yoga-Sastra, 383p.

45. *Ibid.,* 502p.

46. *Ibid.,* 344p.

47. *Ibid.,* 345p.

48. *Ibid.,* 560p.

49. *Ibid.,* 515p.

50. A Step in the Steamer, 76p.

51. *Ibid.,* 71-72.

52. *Ibid.,* 76p.

53. *Ibid.,* 71p.

54. Tilak BG. His Writings and Speeches, 246p.

55. Quoted in Varma VP. "Political Philosophy of Lokmanya Tilak", in Verinder Grover, ed., Political Thinkers of Modern India: Bal Gangadhar Tilak, 18-19.

56. Inamdar NR. "The Political Ideas of Lokmanya Tilak", in Thomas Pantham & Kenneth L. Deutsch, ed., Political Thought in Modern India, 114p.

57. Sreekumaran Nair MP. "Bal Gangadhar Tilak: The Moderate as Extremist", in Verinder Grover, *op. cit.,* 446p.

58. A Step in the Steamer, 41p.

59. *Ibid.,* 113p.

60. Samagra Lokamanya Tilak, 7:265p.

61. All about Lokamanya Tilak, 115p.

62. A Step in the Steamer, 182p.

63. Bakshi SR. Swaraj as Birth Right: Role of Tilak and Annie Besant, 31p.

64. A Step in the Steamer, 66p.

65. Samagra Lokamanya Tilak, 7:265p.

66. A Step in the Steamer, 61p.

67. Samagra Lokamanya Tilak, 7:265p.

68. Inamdar NR. "The Political Ideas of Lokmanya Tilak", in Thomas Pantham & Kenneth L. Deutsch, eds., Political Thought in Modern India, 115p.

69. Jayashree B Gokhale. "The Mahratta' and Nationalism in Maharashtra", the Indian Political Science Review. 1975; 9(1):2p.

70. Inamdar NR. "The Political Ideas of Lokmanya Tilak", in Thomas Pantham & Kenneth L. Deutsch, *op. cit.,* 117p.

71. Athalye DV. The Life of Lokamanya Tilak (Poona: Annasahib Chiploonkar), 1921, 349-50.

72. Tilak BG. His Writings and Speeches, 377p.

73. Samagra Lokmanya Tilak, 7:530p.

74. A Step in the Steamer, 168p.

75. Quoted in Inamdar NR. "The Political Ideas of Lokmanya Tilak", in Thomas Pantham & Kenneth L. Deutsch, *op. cit.,* 119p.

76. Tilak BG. His Writings and Speeches, 77p.

77. Quoted in M.P. Sreekumaran Nair, "Bal Gangadhar Tilak: The Moderate as Extremist" in Verinder Grover, *op. cit.,* 447p.

78. *Ibid.,* 448p.

79. Das HH, Patro PSN. Indian Political Traditions, (Bangalore: Sterling Publications), 1988, 122p.

80. Ravinder Kumar. ed., Selected Documents of Lokamanya Bal Gangadhar Tilak. 1:34p.

81. *Ibid.,* 146p.

82. Samagra Lokamanya Tilak. 7:530p.

83. Inamdar NR. "The Political Ideas of Lokmanya Tilak", in Thomas Pantham & Kenneth L. Deutsch, *op.cit,* 119p.

84. Varma VP. "Political Philosophy of Lokamanya Tilak", in Verinder Grover, *op.cit,* 26p.

85. Tilak BG. His Writings and Speeches, 301p.

86. Sri Aurobindo, Bande Mataram: Early Political Writings-I, (Pondicherry: Sri Aurobindo Ashram). 1972; 1:98p.

87. *Ibid.,* 124p.

88. Gandhi MK. Hindu Dharma (Ahmedabad: Navjivan Publishing House), 1958, 140p.

89. Nirmal Kumar Bose, Selections from Gandhi (Ahmedabad: Navajivan Publishing House), 1948, 142-43.

90. Chidambaram Pillay VD, in Bapat SV. ed., Reminiscences and Anecdotes of Lokamanya Tilak, (Poona: S.V. Bapat). 1928; 3:161-62.

91. Kelkar NC. Life and Times of Lokamanya Tilak, 65p.

92. Varma VP. The Life and Philosophy of Lokamanya Tilak, 65p.

93. *Ibid.,* 66p.

94. Varma VP. "Political Philosophy of Lokamanya Tilak", in Verinder Grover, *op.cit,* 19p.

95. Bapat SV. Reminiscences and Anecdotes of Lokamanya Tilak, 2:204p.

96. *Ibid.,* 3:36-37.

97. *Ibid.,* 218p.

98. Tilak BG. quoted in Karmarkar DP. Bal Gangadhar Tilak: A Study (Bombay: Popular Book Depot), 1956, 165p.

99. Varma VP. Modern Indian Political Thought, *op.cit,* 222p.

100. Sri Aurobindo. Karmayogin: Early Political Wrilings-2, (Pondicherry: Sri Aurobindo Ahsram). 1972; 2:42p.

101. Nirmal Kumar Bose, Selections from Gandhi, 43p.

Chapter - 4

Tilak's Concept of Swaraj

Lokamanya Tilak's life was full of dynamic activities. He was a man of indomitable courage and optimism. He was the first national leader from Maharashtra and was regarded as "Lion of Maharashtra", "Father of Indian Unrest" and the spokesman of the political radicals. He dominated the Indian political scene for about three decades. The greatest asset in life was his strong moral character. His courage was invincible, his attitude was firm and bold. He never despaired, never lost his heart, nor did he fear anybody. He struggled throughout his life for the attainment of freedom of the nation. Self-rule or swaraj became an important objective of his life.

Tilak talked of swaraj as early as 1885 [1] and traced the word swarajyam. in shastras. He often reminded the people that the idea of swaraj was an old one. The term was perhaps as old as the Aryan civilization and it was found in the Rig-veda and the Hindu Shastras.

Tilak referred to swaraj's spiritual and moral meaning, although he did it only on a few occasions. In the spiritual sense swaraj meant self-realisation or the realisation of spiritual inner freedom. Swaraj in the spiritual sense, according to Tilak, could be obtained by the combination of spiritual knowledge and desireless action.

Lokamanya Tilak was a great Vedantist. He believed in the advaita philosophy. According to it, all men are portions or aspects of the Absolute and hence all have the same autonomous spiritual potentialities. The spirit was considered the supreme reality and men as portions or aspects of the absolute essence, hence all have the same autonomous spiritual potentialities. Tilak argued that the individual and the supreme soul were one and that the ultimate goal of the soul was liberation or Swaraj. As he said, "Freedom is the very life of the individual soul which Vedanta declares to be not separate from God but identical with Him. Thus freedom was a principle that could never perish" [2].

According to Tilak, spiritual freedom or swaraj could be achieved by spiritual knowledge. Spiritual knowledge meant the realisation of the identity of the Brahman and Atman. To quote him, "attaining the knowledge of the true Paramesvara, that is, realising the identity of the Brahman and Atman and that there is only one Atman in all created beings and behaving accordingly, is the climax of Spiritual knowledge" [3].

Although Tilak was basically a proponent of Advaita Vedanta, he differed from the classical Advaitin view that Jnana (knowledge) alone brings release. Tilak was impressed by the fact that Bhaktiyoga and Jnanayoga were subservient to Karma preached in the Gita. He preferred the doctrine of "Karmayoga" which he believed to be the central idea of the Gita. Tilak's interpretation in stressing disinterested action (Karma) rather than quietism or ascetic renunciation (sanyasa) or devotion (bhakti) as the central esoteric teaching of the Gita differed basically from earlier mainstreams of Vedantist philosophy. To quote him, "the Karma-Yoga is superior to the Path of Renunciation it will be impossible for us to abandon Karma, so long as the world in which we live, as also our very existence in it for even a single moment, is itself Karma; and if one has to live in this world, that is to say, in this land of Action, how can one escape Action?" [4]

Tilak believed in "Karma Jyaohyakarmanah" (i.e. "Action is superior to inaction") which had been enunciated in the Gita [5].

He basically developed the thesis that proper action was the high road to salvation (Swaraj). The man who performed such action truly understood the mystic knowledge of the identity of the real self (atman) with the transcendent universal principle (Brahman). "That man is the truly learned man" wrote Tilak, "who is the doer" [6].

In a speech delivered at Amraoti in 1917 he said that the conclusion he had came to was that the Gita advocated the performance of action in this world even after the actor had achieved the highest union with the supreme Deity by Gyana (knowledge) or Bhakti (devotion) [7].

Life itself is an energy whose very nature is activity and to pretend to give it up is less than honest. So activity has to be undertaken and if so it must be done without addiction to its fruit. Tilak had been a Karmayogin throughout his life and always endeavoured hard to achieve final liberation of human mind. He stressed that it would be difficult to achieve swaraj by remaining without action and Karmayoga was important to attain swaraj. To quote him, "Karmayoga or to put it another way, the law of Duty is the combination of all that is best in spiritual science, in actual action and in an unselfish meditative life. Compliance with this universal law leads to the realization of the most cherished ideals of man. Swaraj is the natural consequence of diligent performance of duty. The Karma Yogin strives for

Swaraj and the Dynamic or spiritualist yearn for it. Karmayoga is nothing but the method which leads to the attainment of Dharma or material and spiritual glory" [8].

Even in his own book, Gita-Rahasya, Tilak rejected the earlier interpretation which had assigned inferior position to Karma, and expounded in a remarkable manner the doctrine of energism. In the Gita-Rahasya, Tilak attempted to prove two contentions. Firstly, that Gita advocated primarily a philosophy of action rather than renunciation or devotion and secondly, that social or political action was the duty of all citizens when the nation was threatened by internal decay or external oppression [9].

According to Tilak, Swaraj in the spiritual sense had bearing on moral connotation of Swaraj. He believed that spiritual good was the basis of social good. He wrote, "The structure of faith collapses with the collapse of faith in the existence of the soul. The doctrine of soulless-ness removed the need for Faith. But when Faith thus ceased to be an organic force binding together, society was bound to be disrupted and individuals living in a community were sure to find their own different paths of happiness. The ties which bind the society in one harmonious organization would be snapped, and no other binding principle would take their place. Moral ties would in loosen, and people would fall from good moral standard [10].

According to Tilak swaraj in its moral connotation meant the attainment of the perfection of self-control which was essential for performing one's duty (Swadharma) and meant the exercise of one's freedom lawfully. It also meant the regulation of all actions morally in accordance with the individual's Swadharma. Unless there was Swadharma, the individual could not live in his true nature. Tilak believed that the regulation of activities morally according to the rule of Dharma was essential, as without it purpose of life and creation could not be fulfilled.

Swaraj was meaningful in the classical philosophy of politics for the political community. Swaraj meant the lawful exercise of the community's freedom. For the community it also meant the choice of cosmos over chaos, and the regulation of all community activities morally in accordance with Dharmarajya, the rule of Dharma. Unless there was Swaraj, the conscious, lawful living under Dharmarajya, the right ordering of the community could never be attained, individual life situations could not be morally profitable, men could not live in their true natures, and the purpose of life and creation could not be fulfilled. The political community existed only to preserve and promote the Dharma, and without Swaraj this was not possible. Swaraj, therefore, in the classical value system was a moral imperative for both the individual and the community. Without Swaraj life was not worthwhile. Because Tilak viewed the world from the perspective of this value system, he insisted that 'our life and our Dharma are in vain in the absence of Swarajya" [11].

Swaraj was moral imperative, as it was the foundation and not the height of future prosperity. He stressed that without Swaraj there was no Dharmarajya and without Dharmarajya there was no harmony neither in the state nor in the society. He stressed that self-rule under Dharmarajya either existed fully or did not exist at all. Partial Swaraj was a contradiction in terms [12].

According to Tilak, swaraj referred to the self-rule of the individual and to self-rule of the political community. It was a part of both, the philosophy of life and the philosophy of politics. To quote him, "It is a life centred in self and dependent upon self. There is swaraj in this world as well as in the world hereafter. The Rishis who laid down the law of duty betook themselves to forests, because the people were already enjoying swarajya or people's dominion which had administered and defended in the first instance by the Kshatriya kings" [13].

It is observed that the dominant metaphysical assumptions of Tilak influenced his political ideas. His political convictions were based on his philosophical foundations and were influenced by Vedanta. Tilak used the Vedantic principle of self-identification as a base for affirming the unity of man with the entire world. To quote him, "If man seeks unity with the Deity, he must necessarily seek unity with the interests of the world also, and work for it. If he does not, then the unity is not perfect, because there is union between two elements out of the 3 (man and Deity) and the third (the world) is left out. I have thus solved the question for myself and I hold that serving the world, and thus serving His will, is the surest way of Salvation, and this way can be followed by remaining in the world and no going away from it" [14].

According to the Vedanta, man had the potentiality to become God himself and Tilak raised the question that if that was true could not the Indians attain self-government? Tilak tried to relate internal swaraj with external swaraj. According to him, there was no conflict between the Vedantic ideals and the patriotic ideals [15].

Thus he contended that spiritual swaraj was not at all different from people's government, and added, "Our religious literature seems to be devoted almost exclusively to the attainment of the spiritual kingdom, chiefly because the material power was already in the possessions of our ancestors; and we must interpret these ancient books in the hght of this explanation" [16].

Tilak argued that according to their religious books swaraj in the spiritual sense could be realised by the desireless performance of our duty. He added, "If this is true in the case of an individual, it must be equally true in the case of a nation" [17]. Thus he contended that man could also realise swaraj in the political sense by performing his duty with a desireless frame of mind.

Tilak asserted that it was strange that the people who were busy trying to achieve bliss in other world held themselves aloof from the struggle of their national freedom. Since the country was under foreign subjection at that time, he laid more stress on the attainment of swaraj in the political sense.

Tilak put forward a positive political programme, which centred around the concept of swaraj or self-rule for India. Talking about swaraj in the political sense he said that the demand that the management of our affairs should be in our hands was the demand for swarajya. To identify true Swaraj, it was necessary to properly understand the meaning of 'Swa' (self). To Tilak, the prefix 'Swa' (self) in Swaraj could only mean 'Praja' the people, the ruled. And hence, according to him, Swaraj meant (the People and the Ruled), People's rule [18].

Tilak argued that when Swarajya was spoken of it showed that there was some kind of rule opposed to swa i.e. ours. He said, "We want equality. We cannot remain slaves under foreign rule. We will not carry for an instant longer, the yoke of slavery that we have carded all these years. Swaraj is our birth-right. We must have it at any cost. When the Japanese, who are Asians like us, are free, why should we be slaves? Why should our Mother's hands be handcuffed" [19]. Tilak defined swaraj as 'People' rule instead of that of bureaucracy. To quote him, "It is simple Sanskrit word, meaning nothing more or less than the power to rule our homes and hence it is called in short 'Home-rule" [20].

Tilak declared that Swaraj, self-rule, Home-rule, self-government and constitutional government etc. were similar terms having the same meaning. As he said, "Let us glance. As I said, ten years ago when Dadabhai Naroroji declared that Swaraj should be our goal, its name was swaraj. Later on it came to be known as self-government or constitutional reform and we nationalists style it Home-rule. It is all the same, in three different names" [21].

Lokamanya Tilak identified swarajya with Home-rule and to him the meaning of both of them was the same. The idea of starting a Home-rule league originated with Mrs. Annie Besant and she announced it on 25th September, 1915. In September, 1915, she made a speech at Bombay **pleading India's case for Home**-rule or self-government in which she said, "I mean by self-government that the country shall have a government by councils, elected by all the people, elected with power of the purse, and the government is responsible to the House" [22].

On 28th April, 1916, Tilak started a home-rule league to propagate swaraj. The objective of Home-rule was attainment of self-government within the British Empire by all constitutional means and to educate and organise public opinion in the country towards the attainment of the same. He demanded self-government strictly on colonial lines and stressed the fact that self-government should be under the aegis of the British government. To quote him, "A very simple definition of Home-Rule which even a peasant would understand is that I should be in my own country what an Englishman is in England" [23].

Tilak justified the demand for Home-rule and argued that it was conceded by the judiciary as well as executive that Home-rule was a proper ambition for any nation to entertain. In a leading article in the Mahratta, explaining the reasons why it became necessary to bring the league into existence, Tilak wrote, "It was generally recognized that the time had positively come for an organization to be started for educating public opinion and agitating for Home-rule throughout the country. The spade work has got to be done by someone. It can afford to wait no longer. The League may be regarded as a pioneer movement and is not intended in any sense to be an exclusive movement" [24].

Home-rule movement marked the beginning of a new phase in India's struggle for freedom. It placed before the country a concrete scheme of self-government. According to Tilak, "Freedom was the soul of the Home-rule Movement. The divine instinct of Freedom never aged. Circumstances might affect .its manifestation on the physical plane; the movements for freedom (the bodies) might be weakened and maimed for time; but ultimately the Soul-Freedom must triumph."[25] He added, "Our ideal is Swaraj, All past ideals are amalgamated into one pure and simple ideal of Swaraj - government for the people, by the people" [26].

However, Tilak was not satisfied with the attainment of self-government only. The other connotations of swaraj recognised by Tilak were that it referred to a well-governed state or a system of rule of law. Moreover, it meant a government promoting the well-being of the people and lastly Tilak had his strongest preference for the government elected by and responsible to the people [27].

Tilak wanted to establish a well-governed state based on rule of law. According to him, the wholesome changes should be brought about in the administration by strictly lawful means. Tilak stressed that no government could continue in power so long as it forfeited it's legitimacy among the masses. He mentioned that as a Raja — government had an authority to punish a person who committed the offence of Rajdroha, the Praja also had moral authority or right to punish the Raja or government for committing the offence of Praja-droha [28]. He believed that king had moral authority to govern till he enjoyed the consent of the people. It seems that Tilak was impressed by Lockean contract theory. According to which, the ruler and the ruled are the product of mutual contract. Tilak's explanation about the mutual obligations of Raja and Praja seem to be similar to that theory.

Thus Tilak asserted that self-government was not sufficient and it should be accompanied by good-government (suraj) which existed for the well-being of all sections of the society. Moreover, Tilak wanted to explore the forces that would make swaraj meaningful in the true sense of the term. He believed that the government's role did not end with the maintenance of law and order in the country. He argued that mere well disciplined state was not sufficient and people should examine how much their opinion was considered by the government in its decision-making process. It was obligatory for the government to realise that the people would be properly fed and protected within the state. According to Tilak, swadeshi government should be responsive to the people's wishes.

However, Tilak perceived the possibility of a swadeshi government turning tyrannical and power-hungry. By citing the examples of Russia under the Czar and Germany under the Kaiser, Tilak argued that Indians should learn from the experience of others that the mere fact that the Raja (Government) was swadeshi could not guarantee the solution of all problems.

In an article, he wrote, "it is not enough to only to have a swadeshi ruler. The more important question is how much power the people possess in the Swaraj and not whether the ruler is indigenious or alien. When we ask our people to make efforts for swaraj, we mean that the people must get political power" [29].

Tilak made a distinction between the visible and invisible government. Though he wanted that the invisible government should remain the same, he wanted change in the visible government. He stressed on the fact that the government should allow them (Indians) to administer their own affairs in accordance with their wishes and the public servants should be responsible to them for their doings. He tried to make this idea clear in a speech delivered by him at Belgaum on I[st] May, 1916. He began his speech by asking the people not to confuse the institution of kingship with the bureaucratic administration of India. To quote him, "just as Brahma is different from Maya. The latter assumes diverse shapes and forms which change according to occasion and circumstances - change is very essence of Maya. The institution of kingship, which is the essence of government, is like the absolute Brahman, bound to remain immutable and unchanged; but the government which assumes the visible form is liable to change but what we demand is that the management of our affairs should not be, as now, in the hands of the visible government - the bureaucracy - but should be transferred to our hands. In one word, the agitation for swaraj is for the transfer of this control to the people of the land" [30].

Tilak aspired for the government elected by and responsible to the people and wanted an active participation of the people in the government of their country. He meant by swaraj a representative government in which the wishes of the people would be respected and acted upon and not disregarded in the interests of a small minority of civil servants. As he said, "Let there be a viceroy and let him be an Englishman if you like, but let him act according to the advice of the representatives of the people" [31].

Tilak endeavoured hard to bring the common man on the political scene of India and extended his efforts to democratise Indian politics. He set India on the path of democracy. Tilak's foresight and democratic spirit was reflected when he said, "It is obligatory on the part of the educated to change the present sorry state of affairs. They ought to make the masses realize that they (the masses) are the real pillars of strength. Likewise, they must be assured (made aware) of their great potential for achievement and be taught to look upon themselves as the 'real' ruler" [32].

Tilak aspired for a 'responsible government', a government where the executive was entirely responsible to the legislature and it should be elected by the people. According to him, whether it should be called by the name of parliament or anything else, but the essential element should be that it should be entirely responsible to the people. He even wanted that governors and lieutenant governors should be elected by legislative bodies.

Tilak clearly visualised how swaraj could be achieved. He wrote, "The authorities have to conduct themselves in subservience to public, in proportion to the rights of Swarajya acquired by the people. That power should remain in the hands of such authorities as may be approved by the people and that it should be taken away from the hands of such authorities as may not be liked by the people; this itself is called (the exercise of) the rights of Swarajya. If Swarajya is exercised there will be no bombs" [33]. He equated swaraj with democratic self-rule and tried to bring this message to the common man in his own language and idiom.

Tilak was convinced that the people would be happy and satisfied under a democratic self-government that grants liberty and freedom to the people. He stated that once the constitutional democratic government was established, it would be difficult to suppress and extinguish the urge for democratic self-rule. He claimed that Russian experience was a living example to this. Tilak's approach to swaraj was dynamic and future oriented. He equated swaraj with democratic self-rule and tried to bring this message to the common man in his own language and idiom. Tilak was convinced that the remedy for spiritual and material deprivation that India had been experiencing was dependent on its regaining swaraj - the inalienable right to shape one's own destiny. He evaluated the overall impact of the 'imperial relationship' on India as a subject country and argued that foreign domination had transformed Indians into mere dwarfs. He took into account the total impact of political subjugation on a subject nation and stressed the fact that every imperial ruler had its own lust for power domination. Tilak pointed out that the interests of any imperial nation and subject nation could not remain compatible to each-other and would necessarily be at variance. He regarded British rule or colonial rule as being inimical to India's progress and asserted that the country suffered severely with daridrya (poverty), dushkal (famine) and drauyashodha (drain). He said, "The Home-Government would be considerate and just, only on the matters of minor importance. It was hoping against hope that Britishers would ever agree to any fundamental changes in the basic features of the British imperial system" [34].

Tilak tried to enlighten the people about evils and economic exploitation under foreign rule. In a speech at the Lahore Congress (1900) in supporting the resolution demanding the institution of an independent inquiry into the economic condition of Indian people, Tilak said, "Howsoever rich a country is and the soil fertile, if the administration is carried on in such a way that you take away from the country a large portion of the produce without returning to it its equivalent in one form or another, in a material form, not in the form of prestige or advice, then, unless you give back to the people in some material form the return for the wealth that you take away from the country, the only natural result of it would be that the country must grow poorer and poorer" [35].

Tilak asserted that the responsibility for economic misery of the people was on the British government itself and condemned the British government for throwing responsibilities on Indians for their economic degradation and miseries.

It goes to the contribution of Tilak for elaborating how India had been reduced to the position of a beast of burden and that foreign rulers were knowingly discriminating between their own white people and Indians. Tilak had strong belief that progress rested on swaraj and no other issue had precedence over swaraj. Thus according to him, swaraj alone was the root of all reforms and all talk of industrial progress, proper education and social reforms were futile without it. He reminded the people that, "In the absence of Swarajya we can make no industrial progress, in the absence of swarajya no useful education - be it primary or higher - can be imparted. It there is no Swarajya, there is no use labouring for the spread of female education, there is no use trying to secure industrial development and social reform also can avail but little. All these reforms form the component parts of swarajya" [36].

Tilak regarded swaraj as the key to the fulfilment of all other demands and said, "When this is acquired, all the subsidiary rights will come into our hands, of themselves. This is the root of the thousand and one demands we have been asking for. Possessed with this key, we can open not only one but several other doors all at once" [37].

Tilak was convinced that no significant social progress was possible in a country that was not politically free. He disagreed with his colleagues on the issue of primacy of social reforms over political change. He believed that the cause of social reform might best be tackled when India would attain swaraj or self-government. According to him, Britishers were responsible for so many social conflicts such as communalism, alcoholism, casteism etc.

Tilak believed that the issue of self-government should not be harnessed to the goal of abolition of caste and other evils in the society, which would take centuries to achieve. He had not visualised the picture of a perfect political society, its features and possibilities and his political thinking narrowed down to a single problem, namely the political emancipation of his country [38].

According to Tilak, reforms had to be carried out by each community and meaningful reform could only take place within the context of a politically free India. He was not bHnd to social evils and injustices and would have never tolerated them in a free India. But he was convinced that the emancipation of the country must have the first priority in his national 40 programme, for without it social reform could make no real headway [39]. Moreover Tilak contended that social reform movement would expose cleavages within Hindu society, whereas the spirit of nationalism would unite the whole country and would provide a practical sphere of action to be realised within a limited time period. At the same time he fought against the schemes of the westernizing reformers and believed that the use of force or legislation by an alien raj to impose any kind of reform would make that reform itself immoral.

Tilak pleaded for swaraj not only for his firm belief that all progress and development depended on it but also because he believed that a free India could play a positive role in promoting peace. He argued that India could play a leading role in maintaining peace in Asia if not in the world. However, swaraj was a necessary condition for that. Thus he said, "it is, therefore, absolutely necessary that India should be self-governed internally, 41 and be made the bulwark of liberty in the East" [40].

Tilak regarded swaraj as an essential necessity of national life and aroused the nationalistic feeling of the people by reminding them about India's past history and civilization. He demanded national freedom for India by talking about it's glorious past and by rejecting the British claim that Indians did not deserve self-rule or swaraj.

Tilak realised that people were living in a state of servitude, despair and apathy and were overpowered by a feeling of inferiority complex. They had completely resigned themselves and their fortunes to British rule and had lost their self-confidence and self-esteem. Tilak struggled to reawaken India to her glorious past and to base her future greatness on her past glories. According to him, awareness must grow jfrom within the people. It would have to be based on the value system of the people and not on the values taught by the westernized few. He talked about the superiority of Indian civilization and argued that, "British statesman themselves have often declared that India was civilised centuries before the modern nations of Europe emerged from barbarism" [41].

To Tilak, it was criminal, to banish everything created by Indian civilization on the ground that Indian values and Indian religion did not coincide with the nineteenth-century European notions of materialism, rationalism and utilitarianism.

Tilak was among the first Indians to make a stand against western civilization and the western influence which had hypnotized all Indians, masses and classes alike. His strategy for attaining political swaraj involved mobilizing the people and generating among them a political awareness. He advocated the necessity of enlightening the masses on their role in sustaining a political set-up.

He was the first leader to take the message of swaraj to the masses through various channels. He was acclaimed as the Lokamanya, the leader revered by the people. By stressing on the glorious history of India, Tilak urged the people to become fearless and courageous enough to aspire for selfrule or swaraj. He regarded swaraj or self-rule as the birthright of every nation and argued that, "no civilized nation should be governed by any other nation without its consent" [42].

Lokamanya Tilak also tried to promote national political consciousness in people by his writings and speeches and by organizing fairs and festivals. It must be added to the credit of Tilak that he realised that to educate the masses, to kindle the love of the country in them, newspapers could play a significant role. He regarded communication with people, their awareness about the problems and role of public opinion very important in this respect and used newspapers very effectively in pursuing the ultimate objective (swaraj). For almost his entire public life, he used newspapers very effectively. Working through Kesari [43] (a Marathi language weekly) and Maratha [44] (it's English language counterpart), he developed a more advanced nationalist perspective. Through his newspapers, the first objective he pursued was the awakening of the people to their heritage of self-rule.

With Chiplunkar, Agarkar and Namjoshi, Tilak launched a nationalist weekly - the Kesari. He used it as an effective media to criticize the British government by writing articles in it. Kesari's every issue carried a message, "Oh: intoxicated elephant: get cleared off this jungle immediately because here in the cave is living a Hon, who can break the big bidders with the help of his paws" [45].

Similarly, Tilak used Kesari as the best organ for the propaganda of his political creed. Through his writings in it, he could influence a major portion of the population in the western region. He apprised the people of their fundamental rights and urged them to prepare themselves for the grim battle of freedom. He wrote that the only way to settle the Indian problem was a proclamation by the king of England declaring that the ultimate object of the British government was to grant swaraj to the people of India [46].

With the help of the Kesari, he brought about the political unity of Maharashtra. Through his writings in it, Tilak endeavoured to inspire the people to get united to attain self-rule or swaraj. As his colleague, N.C. Kelkar wrote, "Through his paper, the Kesari, he exercised an immense influence over the masses, and it is this influence that is mainly responsible for the infusion of a new spirit among the people" [47].

Looking at the rude behaviour of the British bureaucracy and police at the time of famine (1896) and atrocities committed by them at the time of plague (1897) in Pune, Tilak spread awareness among the masses by writing fearlessly about it. He condemned the inhuman aspects of the British anti-plague campaign.

His writings especially in 'Kesari' also resulted in his imprisonment. Thus Tilak found an effective media to spread awareness of the various issues about which Indians were ignorant. He also used Kesari to spread the message of national importance of Shivaji and Ganesh festivals among the masses.

Through Maratha Tilak developed a more advanced nationalist perspective. The Maratha intended to interpret what the educated Indian community thought on matters pertaining to British rule and to present this opinion in as candid a way as possible. It intended to become an all-India paper, read by English educated men and women all over India. Through Maratha, Tilak expanded his area of influence to spread the message of swaraj to each and every section of the society. His sincerity and unflinching sense of dedication led him to champion the cause of his people against any and all who would be unjust, autocratic or opportunistic.

Tilak used this English newspaper as an effective means to unite the linguistically diversified Indian society for spreading the message of swaraj or self-rule. Similarly, through his effective writings he tried to incite the feelings of general masses against the ineffective policy making and policy implementation.

It must go to the credit of Tilak that he was the first Maharashtrian leader to bridge the gap between the elite Indian National Congress and the more traditional masses through his writings. He further stressed that it was the duty of leaders of the Indian National movement to prepare the nation for a struggle for swaraj. Tilak stressed in his various writings in newspapers that objectives of Indian freedom struggle could be fulfilled only when the common people, represented by the vast majority of peasants, artisans and workers were initiated to participate in the struggle for the attainment of swaraj.

He also used traditional fairs and festivals for enlightening the countrymen about the tyranny of the British government. He regarded traditional fairs and festivals as the most effective means of approaching the masses and uniting them under one umbrella. As in the Indian context, Tilak was to make a dent on the political apathy of the people and had to orient them to the national movement for attaining swaraj. In this direction he started Shivaji and Ganesh festivals to kindle the spirit of nationalism.

Lokamanya Tilak not only initiated the festivals of Shivaji and Ganesh, but also essentially tried to make them viable platform for enunciation of the national sentiments and thereby arousing the sleeping masses of the nation through his vibrant speeches delivered in these festivals. He endeavoured to inculcate the values of liberty, freedom and self-government. He hoped for getting immense support from the masses by rationalizing his stand on the concept of swaraj which would get universal acceptance.

Tilak started Shivaji celebrations in Maharashtra in 1895 to give his political activities a national turn by arousing the sentiments of the people around a national hero. The inauguration of the Shivaji festival had it's origin in the attitude of hero-worship borrowed by him from Carlyle and Ruskin [48]. He believed that the "heroes" were the creators of History. It was their great work which inspired the ordinary man and gave him ideals to aim at. Tilak found in Shivaji a hero. In Maharashtra, Shivaji and swarajya were the two sides of coin [49].

Tilak thought that through Shivaji festival the agitation for swaraj would reach the masses more quickly than by other means. He was influenced by the valour and courage of great Shivaji and the glorious history of Maratha, their war against the atrocities of Mughal Empire to restore swaraj and dharma. In this regard he said, "One who is a wee bit introduced to history and knows what is swaraj (People's own government) and Swadharma (People's own religion) knows the extraordinary qualities that are needed for the founder to establish Swaraj and Swadharma when both of them are in a state of ruin for hundreds of years, knows the valour, courage, guts and brains of Shivaji Maharaja, by the dint of which he saved the whole nation from bitter ruin" [50].

According to Tilak, Shivaji was a national hero and at a time when national qualities of solidarity, patriotism, hatred of tyranny were absent, he wanted to make an appeal to the people by involving the memory of the glorious times of the great national hero. In pursuance of this idea, he organized the first Shivaji celebration which was a great success and the villagers from all over Maharashtra had gathered at the place, some of them walking several miles [51]. He continued to organise Shivaji festival to arouse wider national consciousness and for the unification of country.

He tried to unite Brahmins and Non-Brahmins together through this festival. He even invited Muslims to take part in the Shivaji festivals for spreading up the movement for attaining self-rule or swaraj. Tilak worked tirelessly to reach the people and to educate them through his speeches and activities. Through his speeches, he urged people from diverse sections of society to come together for attaining the ultimate objective (swaraj). Shivaji festival was started in Maharashtra with the hope that it would spread all over India.

Similarly, he introduced Ganesh festival in 1893 to revive the sleeping spirit of patriotism and nationalism for attaining the highest objective (swaraj). Tilak tried to use the religious fervour of the people for political purposes by celebrating the Ganapati festival. From his study of Greek history he had learnt how Olympian Games had developed into a great national festival which built-up a national spirit among the many independent city states of Greece. Every fourth year, a religious festival in honour of God Jupiter was held in the plain of Olympia, with sacrifices, processions and games, while poets and authors recited their compositions and artists displayed their works. The Olympian Games thus gradually became a bond of union for all the Greeks, linking them together in peace and love of their country [52]. In an article entitled "The Need of National festival", Tilak referred to the part played by them in Greece and Rome.

He found in the Ganesh festival a "powerful engine for imparting instructions to the masses" which were, he said, "our ultimate court of appeal" [53]. He argued:

> In India, religion will always be regarded as of primary importance and as such our celebrations will naturally have a religious colour. Formerly such occasions were used for keeping the religious sense alive and to give ethical, social and political education to the people. In the time of Vedas, the great sacrifices were in the nature of national celebrations. Such festivals were revived by saint Ramdas in the days of Shivaji. It is the duty of the educated people, therefore, to take an active part in these celebrations instead of lecturing on Bhakti or uttering the name of God behind closed doors [54].

In an article in Kesari (8th September, 1896) entitled as "The Ganesh Festival", Tilak tried to show as to how the religious fervour of the people could be channelized for promoting political ends. He said, "The aims of such national festivals are the two-fold aims of entertainment and public education. They are ways devised by our ancestors to keep-up the religious faith of the people, to vitalize the ethical and political life of the people and to keep the flame of our nationalism burning bright" [55].

Ganapati celebrations were held in all parts of Maharashtra and the people from all communities took part in them. These festivals provided cheapest means of varied entertainment and besides they were used as a ground for political propaganda, as Tilak had envisaged. Tilak had succeeded in bringing together the masses through the Ganapati festival and had succeeded in modernizing them to a certain extent. There is an interesting point in favour of Tilak's selection of the Ganapati festival in preference to many other possible festivals in the Hindu calendar. The climax of Ganapati festival was the immersion of the tabuts, which took place at the end of the Muslim festival of Moharram. This shows that Tilak, far from being inimical to the Muslim sentiments, was very considerate towards Muslims rituals. Thus the basic idea behind initiating these festivals was to unite the whole nation for attaining self-rule or swaraj.

The Ganesh and Shivaji festivals helped him in bringing the politically conscious class in direct contact with the masses. Tilak endeavoured to make the Indian national movement people oriented through these festivals. He used Hindu symbols because Hindus had a mindset to accept things on religious format only and that included politics. The only way to bring Hindus together was through fairs and festivals. For example, in Maharashtra, he used myths and symbols that wotdd appeal to Maharashtrians: the Shivaji festival and Ganapati festival. In the process of trying to develop a national consciousness, regional sentiments were mobilized [56].

However his attitude aroused misgiving among many of the moderates. Ranade, Gokhale and Surendranath Bannerjee not only viewed with alarm the violence of his language but also began to suspect that he spoke and acted first as a Brahman, second as a Maratha and only incidentally as a man with vision of a united India of the future [57].

Tilak was portrayed as anti-Muslim by the Muslim league and misrepresented as a sectarian Hindu revivalist by some historians. As an English journalist wrote, "In these festivals religious songs are sung, dramas are played in which quotes from the Hindu mythology are used to foment hatred against the aliens. A very derogatory term 'Malechch' is used for the Europeans and Muslims. The aim of the festivals is to find excuses to use violence against Muslims and the police which results in court trials. Then, the trials are used to deliver fiery speeches to incite the people. With the beginning of these festivals Tilak's area of influence widens and becomes stronger" [58]. Tilak appealed to the Muslim brethren not to believe in this statement. He regarded it as a trick of the Britishers to divide Hindus and Muslims.

Lokamanya Tilak's politics rested on four principles - swaraj Swadeshi, boycott and national education. He strongly believed that Swadeshi aimed at making people self-reliant and capable of resisting the government that was ruining India. It meant self-help, to rely upon Indian made goods rather than the foreign made products.

According to Tilak, all the self-employing industries of India like spinning, weaving, glass-making, sugar dying and paper making were destroyed by the Britishers. Even economic resources were looted by them. He realised that mere protest against British rule was not going to help and insisted on native production and reliance. Tilak strongly felt that self-reliance was very significant for attaining swaraj and that self-reliance could be attained only by adoption of swadeshi in their lives.

Tilak appealed the people to use only Indian goods and clothes. He even himself used swadeshi paper for the Indian goods and clothes. He even himself used swadeshi paper for the Kesari and the Maratha as far as possible. A big 'Swadeshi Market' was opened in front of Tilak's house. Swadeshi goods were sold in the fifty odd stalls of the Market.

However, Tilak regarded swadeshi not only an industrial movement, but it was also concerned with politics. He asserted that swadeshism was alarge term which included all lines whether industrial, political and economical. To quote him, "Swadeshism is a large term which includes politics and to be a true Swadeshi, one must look on all lines - whether political or industrial or economical which converge our people towards the status of civilized nation" [59].

Tilak chose to communicate with the people in their own language and addressed them in their own idioms. He focused on adopting native and local symbols to inspire people and for making them ready to sacrifice everything for attaining swaraj. Thus according to him, swadeshi was a means of inculcating the patriotic spirit among the people.

The objective of swadeshi was not only to bring about swadeshi goods and the disappearance of foreign products but also to bring about the gradual disappearance of foreign ideas. Thus Tilak added, "Like the bodies our minds also should become swadeshi... Swadeshi thoughts should always reign in our hearts" [60]. It particularly aimed at making India self-reliant in all respect.

Tilak not only propagated the need of self-reliance but also elaborated the concept of self-reliance by advocating that self-reliance was equivalent to involvement and participation of the masses in the freedom struggle. It is observed that Tilak's expectation about Swadeshi proved correct and with it the struggle started to spread from classes to masses.

In a critical political situation of India, Tilak felt that Swadeshism should be used as a pressure upon the alien and unrepentant bureaucracy. Tilak had strong conviction that once a feeling of patriotic self-reliance was aroused, the people would be ready to undergo any sacrifice. The swadeshi movement quickly became a movement of national regeneration. It became a movement for the liberation of the spiritual energies of the nation for the sake of the political emancipation of the land. It was a practical application of love of country. As Tilak said, "To recognize the land of the Aryas as mother-earth is the swadeshi movement" [61].

Tilak further argued that Swadeshi was not possible without boycott. He related swadeshi and boycott and considered them as the two sides of the same coin. According to him, the term boycott expressed the very rationale behind swadeshi. Tilak believed that the people should be aware of the fact that they could make the administration impossible by not cooperating with the Britishers. The power of self-denial and self-abstinence should be there for not assisting foreign government to rule over Indians. According to him, failing to do that would clearly mean that the period of India's misfortune was not yet over.

Tilak believed that boycott was a strong political weapon and regarded it to be stronger and effective than arms for attaining swaraj. He attached greater importance to boycott as a means of exercising pressure on Britain to compel them to grant legitimate rights to Indians. According to him, to rebel against government illegally was an offence, but a boycott was not. He added, "People have not yet developed adequate strength to destroy British rule and to establish Swaraj; but it is possible to make administration deplorably difficult and to create conditions impossible for the British Bureaucracy, by fighting for our rights with determination and tenacity and by boycott and strikes. It has been well said that freedom's struggle once begun, is never lost, but ever won" [62].

Boycott initially involved the refusal of the people to purchase British manufactured goods. It was designed to bring economic pressure on the British business interests both in India and abroad. Tilak was one of the first to discern that the British system of rule over India was based upon the willing, or at least unthinking, cooperation of the Indian people. He realized that boycott could be expanded to the point of jeopardizing the foundation of the whole British administration in India. He tried to revive the spirit of people by reminding them that they were behind the British government and administration. As early as 1902, he declared publicly, "you must realise that you are a great factor in the power with which the administration in India is conducted. You are yourselves the useful lubricants which enable the gigantic machinery to work so smoothly" [63].

Tilak cautioned the people that, they must be conscious of the power of making the administration impossible if they decided to do so. He asserted that the people themselves managed the railroads and the telegraphs, collected revenue and did everything for the administration and they must consider whether they could not turn their hand to better use for their nation than drudging on in that fashion.

The Swadeshi-boycott movement was a mighty attempt at vindicating the rights of the people to self-government, and hence, it perfected several technics of political agitation as, mass processions, big public meetings, strikes, picketing etc.; which have been followed by the later Indian leaders in their political movements [64]. Thus the Swadeshi-boycott movement was an organized attempt for the assertion of the great democratic principle, that the predominant political opinion of the inhabitants of a country must not be transgressed by the rulers.

Lokamanya Tilak talked of boycott and Swadeshi as the techniques of passive resistance. The essence of the method was that the people should refuse in an organised way to do anything that might help the government, and thereby, make the administration impossible. Passive-resistance was a determination to achieve their goal at any sacrifice. As he said, "If they wanted to reach their goal and if they were hindered by artificial and unjust legislation and by any unjust combination of circumstances it was their duty to fight it out. If they did not want to use the words "passive-resistance" they might use the phrase 'at all sacrifices', but he would use both phrases in the same sense in which he explained them" [65].

He regarded passive-resistance perfectly constitutional. Distinguishing between the legal and the constitutional he said, "Law and constitution are not the same. That is proved by history. So long as a particular law is not inconformity with justice and morality and popular opinion, according to the ethics of the 19th and 20th centuries, so long as a particular order is not consistent with all these principles, it might be legal 68 but not constitutional" [66]. Tilak regarded passive-resistance as an effective means of attaining swaraj. According to him, by passive-resistance British government could be pressurized to grant political independence or swaraj to Indians.

Tilak hoped for envisaging the new spirit of self-help and self-dependence through national education. Tilak believed that national education identifies oneself with one's own nation. He regarded the education system of that time as a failure because it had failed to inspire the people. However, Tilak's advocacy of national education did not mean that he had failed to appreciate the relevance and significance of modern western education and knowledge. As he observed, "Because of their tendency to indulge into formal semantic debates, the scholarship in the traditional Indian disciplines such a Nyaya, Vyakarana etc. though sharpened the intellectual faculty, did not, materially, enhance the knowledge of 'Life Sciences' that facilitates progress of a nation. By life sciences are meant subjects like spirit of nationalism, a sense of obligation to the 'motherland', system of government, theory of politics, issues concerning moral and material development of the nation, inter-relationship between nations etc" [67].

Tilak talked about certain essential ingredients of national education. According to him, first of all, religious education should be promoted. He said that religious education was necessary because the study of high principles keep us away from evil pursuits. Secondly he proposed that education should be imparted through vernaculars, and the load of study of foreign languages should be reduced. Thirdly, he laid stress on industrial education and finally he argued that there should be education in politics to make the people aware of their political rights.

Thus Tilak considered national education very important to inculcate the spirit of nationalism and patriotism for the attainment of self-rule or swaraj. He believed that a nation which did not take its education in its own hand could not rise in literacy, social and political independence.

Similarly, Tilak regarded common language necessary for uniting the linguistically divided India for attaining swaraj. He said, "If you want to draw a nation together, there is no force more powerful than a common language for all" [68]. In this scheme English had no place and he urged its replacement by Hindi.

Tilak exhorted the people to use legitimate means for the attainment Swaraj or Self-rule. He said, "I do not preach unruliness or illegality" [69]. However, he added that it rested with the government whether to make their agitation legal or illegal. He explained that as law-making was not in their hands a movement which was legal at present could be made illegal by the government in future. He argued that such laws could be passed which were opposed to justice and morality and asserted that the people could not obey such laws. According to him, under such circumstances their agitation should be guided by justice and morality. Tilak asked people to go beyond the three P's - Prayers, Pleas and Petitions.

Adoption of violent and non-violent means for the attainment of swaraj was an another major issue. Tilak highly appreciated the principle of non-injury (ahimsa) and emphasised that principle had been accepted as pre-eminent not only in their Vedic religion but in all other religions. He went on to offer the definition of himsa and ahimsa by stating that hinsa did not mean only destroying life but also included harming the minds and bodies of others. Therefore, ahmisa meant not harming in any way any living being [70].

From Tilak's standpoint ahimsa was an absolute and unquestionable principle at the stage of Moksha-dharma. Yet even sthitaprajnas who had reached the equable state of mind must not, living in this world, abstain from retaliation. He said, "The Gita neither advices nor intends that when one becomes non-inimical (this is attained in the process of realising the Oneness of Atman in all living things - I. ch.), one should also become non retaliatory" [71].

Tilak never advocated absolute non-violence as a means for attaining swaraj. He supported the action of Shivaji in killing Afzal Khan and he also appreciated the patriotic fervour of the Bengal revolutionaries. Tilak and the revolutionaries were, in a sense, nearer to each other. Both of them had refused to accept the British rulers as 'Political Gurus'. Also, it must be understood, Tilak had not totally eschewed the idea of using violent revolutionary methods.

It is certain that Tilak did not glorify violence per se. He maintained that, as far as possible, "One should, if possible, resist an evil-minded person through pious means. Evil need not necessarily be answered by evil. If, however, one cannot contain evil with piety, one should not hesitate to adhere to even harsh or ruthless means" [72]. Tilak gave an apt simile: "When simple, painless medicines fail, one has to take resort to a needle for removing a thorn embedded in one's flesh" [73]. He further emphasized that a vicious person loses the moral right "to expect others to behave righteously with him" [74]. "Moreover", Tilak observed, "the Dharmashastras maintain that for the lapse of righteousness on the part of the pure-minded saintly person, not the saintly person but the vicious person who compels the former to commit such an act should be held morally responsible" [75]. Tilak extended the same logic to the freedom struggle. He suggested that, in this imperfect world, whether the methods used in any freedom struggle are violent or nonviolent need not be made a moral issue.

Tilak did not personally advocate either petitioning or violence as a means for the attainment of swaraj. However, he argued that each individual should promote the cause of swaraj in his own way according to his temperament. To quote him:

> Our country is a vast one. In it there are men of different kinds of tendencies and temperaments. Some say that Swaraj can be obtained by petitions, prayers and protest, while some others say that Swaraj cannot be obtained by all these means. Some say that Swaraj can be obtained by doing away with the heads of the Executive Government, while some others say that only persecution wotdd follow such acts. Some say that Swaraj can be attained by a simultaneous revolution throughout the country, while some others say that anarchy would be the result. Some say that Swaraj can be obtained by a war with the help of another country, while some others say that the country would continue to be a slave under that another country, even if it come out successful in war. Let each patriot do what he deems best for his country. Let not others put obstacles in his way. There is room in our country for different kinds of men and for different kinds of activities. One need not clash with the other. Let all acts of construction go on, whatever they and their forms may be. Let no one be disheartened by his failures and sufferings in the course of his work to attain swaraj. Failures will bring knowledge and success [76].

On the basis of preceding discussion it can be argued that swaraj was a passion of Tilak's life. The last word uttered by him on his death-bed pertain to swaraj. He became unquestioned leader of the Indians and was known as the Tilak Maharaj. It is rightly said that Tilak's demand of swaraj was completely consistent with his personal, social and political philosophy. He was a realist and analysed all developments very practically. Even Tilak's life long opponents stated that if Tilak had been born a hundred and twenty years earlier, he would had carved out a kingdom for himself. Pt. Nehru had pointed out that the real symbol of the new age was Bal Gangadhar Tilak and the vast majority of politically minded people in India favoured him.

Tilak's death in 1920 brought Mahatma Gandhi on the scene and Gandhi gave a concrete shape to some of Tilak's ideas. On his death Gandhi wrote in the Young India, "Lokamanya Bal Gangadhar Tilak is no more. The voice of the lion is hushed. His patriotism was a passion with him. He knew no religion but love for his country. He was a born democrat. For us he will go down for posterity as a maker of modern India. They will revere his memory as a man who lived for them and died for them. Let us erect for the only Lokamanya of India an imperishable monument by weaving into our own lives his bravery, his simplicity, his wonderful industry and his love for his country. May God grant peace to his soul" [77].

Gandhi asserted that Tilak used his steel like will power for attaining swaraj. He was an architect of new India. Future generations would remember Tilak with reverence, as the man who lived and died for their sake. In the succeeding chapter an attempt has been made to explore Gandhi's views on swaraj.

Refrences

1. Athalya DV. The Life of Lokamanya Tilak (Poona: Chiploonkar), 1921, 304p.
2. Jose PK. "Gandhi and Tilak: Values in Conflict", Gandhi Marg. 1989; 2(1):51p.
3. Suneera Kapoor. Sri Aurodindo Ghosh and Bal Gangadhar Tilak: The Spirit of Freedom (New Delhi: Deep & Deep Publications), 1991, 97p.
4. Bal Gangadhar Tilak, *OM-TAT-SAT* Srimad Bhagavadgita - Rahasya Karma-Yoga - Sastras (Poona: Lokamanya Tilak Mandir, Narayan Peth), 1965, 440-441.
5. Irina Chelysheva, Ethical Ideas in the World Outlook of Swami Viueakananda, Lokamanya B.G. Tilak and Aurobindo Ghosh (Calcutta: VOSTOK AC - 210, Saltlake), 1989, 60p.
6. Stanley A Wolpert. Tilak and Gokhale: Revolution and Reform in the Making of Modern India (Delhi: Oxford University Press), 1961, 260p.
7. Ravindra Kumar. ed., Selected Documents of Lokamanya Bal Gangadhar Tilak (1880-1920), (New Delhi: Anmol Publications). 1920; 3:59p.
8. *Ibid.,* 64-65.
9. Mackenzie Brown D. "The Philosophy of Bal Gangadhar Tilak: Karma vs. Jnana in the Gita Rahasya" in Verinder Grover, ed., Bal Gangadhar Tilak: Political Thinkers of Modern India-IV (New Delhi: Deep & Deep Publication), 1992, 4p.

10. Theodore L Shay. The Legacy of the Lokamanya: The Political Philosophy of Bal Gangadhar Tilak (London: Oxford University Press), 1956, 58p.

11. *Ibid.,* 100p.

12. *Ibid.,* 104p.

13. Tilak BG. His Writings and Speeches (Madras: Ganesh & Co.), 1919, 245p.

14. Naveen Kumar Sharma. Lokamanya Tilak (New Delhi: Mahaveer & Sons), 2007, 70p.

15. Samagra Lokamanya Tilak, (Poona: Kesari Prakashan). 1976; 7:548p.

16. A Step in the steamer. (Bombay: The National Bureau), 1918, 71-72.

17. *Ibid.,* 73p.

18. Shanta Sathe. Lokamanya Tilak: His Social and Political Thoughts (Delhi: Ajanta Publications), 1994, 74p.

19. Singh MK. Encyclopedia of Great Indian Political Thinkers: Bal Gangadhar Tilak, (New Delhi: Anmol Publications, Pvt. Ltd.). 2008; 3:43p.

20. Tilak BG. His Writings and Speeches, 245p.

21. Bakshi SR. Swaraj as Birth right: Role of Tilak and Annie Besant (Delhi: Vista International Publishing House), 2006, 93p.

22. Majumdar RC. Struggle for Freedom (Bombay: Bhartiya Vidya Bhavan), 1969, 250p.

23. Jog NG. Lokamanya Bal Gangadhar Tilak, (New Delhi: Publication Division, Ministry of Information and Broadcasting, Govt, of India), 1974, 144p.

24. Majumdar RC. Struggle for Freedom, 252p.

25. Suneera Kapoor. "The Idea of Nationalism: A Study in the Political Thought of Tilak, Aurobindo and Gandhi", Gandhian Perspective. 1996; 9(1):29p.

26. Ashok S. Chousalkar, Indian Idea of Political Resistance: Aurobindo, Tilak, Gandhi and Ambedkar (Delhi: Ajanta Publications), 1990, 51p.

27. Inamdar NR. "The Political Ideas of Lokamanya Tilak" in Thomas Pantham & Kenneth L. Deutsch, ed., Political Thought in Modern India

(London: Sage Publications), 1986, 114p.

28. Shanta Sathe. Lokmanya Tilak: His Social and Political Thoughts, 72p.
29. Parvate TV. Bal Gangadhar Tilak (Ahmedabad: Navajivan Publishing House), 1958, 270p.
30. Appadorai A. Documents of Political Thought in Modern India, (Delhi: Oxford University Press). 1973; 1:155-156.
31. Ravindra Kumar. ed., Selected Documents of Lokamanya Tilak, 3:47p.
32. Shanta Sathe. Lokmanya Tilak: His Social and Political Thoughts, 1973, 11p.
33. Reisner IM, Goldberg NM. Tilak and the Struggle for Indian Freedom (New Delhi: People's Publishing House), 1966, 558p.
34. Shanta Sathe. Lokmanya Tilak: His Social and Political Thoughts, 25p.
35. Varma VP. The Life and Philosophy of Lokamanya Tilak (Agra: Lakshmi Narain Agarwal Educational Publishers), 1978, 140p.
36. A Step in the Steamer, 156p.
37. *Ibid.*, 109p.
38. Jose PK. "Gandhi and Tilak: Values in Conflict", Gandhi Marg, *op. cit.*, 51p.
39. Tahmankar DV. Lokamanya Tilak: Father of Indian Unrest and Maker of Modern India (London: John Murray), 1956, 321p.
40. Samagra Lokamanya Tilak. 7:265p.
41. *Ibid.*, 266p.
42. *Ibid.*, 265p.
43. *Kesari* came into publication on 22nd October, 1887.
44. *Maratha* came into publication on 3rd September, 1891.
45. Ashok S Chousalkar. Indian idea of political resistance: Aurobindo, Tilak, Gandhi and Ambedkar, 43p.
46. Bakshi SR. Swaraj as birth right: Role of Tilak and Annie Besant, 42p.
47. Kelkar NC. Landmarks in Lokamanya's Life (Madras; Ganesan & Company), 1924, 10p.
48. Hari Hara Das. Indian Political Thought (New Delhi: National Publishing House), 2005, 156p.

49. Tahmankar DV. Lokamanya Tilak: Father of Indian Unrest and Maker of Modern India, 64p.

50. Hari Hara Das. Indian Political Thought, 171p.

51. Arti, Indian Nationalism and Tilak: A Critical Analysis (New Delhi: National Book Organisation), 1999, 61p.

52. Tahmankar. Lokamanya Tilak: Father of Indian Unrest and Maker of Modern India, 60-61.

53. *Ibid.,* 61p.

54. Arti. Indian Nationalism and Tilak: A Critical Study, 65p.

55. *Ibid.,* 66p.

56. Jayashree B Gokhale. “The Mahratta and nationalism in Maharashtra”, The Indian Political Science Review. 1975; 9(l):11p.

57. Rushbrook Williams LF. ed., Great men of India (Ceylon: The Home Library Club, n.d.), 256p.

58. Vinod Tiwari. Bal Gangadhar Tilak (Delhi: Manoj Publications), 2008, 46p.

59. Arti. Indian Nationalism and Tilak A Critical Analysis, 105p.

60. Naveen Kumar Sharma. Lokamanya Tilak, 92p.

61. *Ibid.*, 93p.

62. Karmarkar DP. Bal Gangadhar Tilak: A Study (Bombay: Popular Book Depot), 1956, 149p.

63. Tilak BG. His Writings and Speeches, 77p.

64. Varma VP. The Life and Philosophy of Lokamanya Tilak (Agra: Lakshmi Narain Aggarwal), 1978, 179p.

65. Tilak BG. His Writings and Speeches, 261p.

66. Samagra Lokmanya Tilak. 7:530-531.

67. Shanta Sathe. Lokamanya Tilak: His Social and Political Thoughts, 52p.

68. Arti. Indian National and Tilak: A Critical Analysis, 76p.

69. Samagra Lokmanya Tilak. 7:530p.

70. Irina Chelysheva. Ethical Ideas in the World outlook of Swami Vivekananda, Lokamanya B.G. Tilak and Aurohindo Ghosh, 78p.

71. *Ibid.*

72. Shanta Sathe. Lokmanya Tilak: His Social and Political Thoughts, 14-

15.

73. *Ibid.*

74. *Ibid.*

75. *Ibid.*

76. Chidambaram Pillay VD, in Bapat SV. ed., *R*eminiscences and Ancedotes of Lokmanya Tilak, (Poona: S.V. Bapat), 1928; 3:161-162.

77. Pradhan GP. Lokamanya Tilak (New Delhi: National Book Trust), 1994, 137p.

Chapter - 5

Conclusion

Although the seeds of nationalism in the form of patriotism in the state of Maharashtra were sown by Chiploonkar, Tilak was the actual founder of a vigorous and valiant nationalism there. Through the newspaper Kesari Lokmanya spread for nearly forty years the gospel of natural rights, political freedom and justice. Tilak taught the residents of Maharashtra the value of organised self help by deciding to serve the plague victims in Poona during the year 1897, he become a leader of the populace who automatically were drawn to him for humanism. Apart from serving the affected people of plague, Tilak wrote several articles in Kesari condemning the arrangement and the steps, the government undertook in fighting this deadly syndrome. The cult of Ganapati and Shivaji gave to the Maratha community a renewed sense of patriotism, vitalism, and the capacity of political self assertiveness. He invigorated the concept of self-rule so called swaraj which was used to designate the polity of Shivaji Maharaj. The inhabitants of Maharashtra thoroughly understood the meaning and message of Tilak. Majority of the Indians regarded Lokmanya Balgangadhar Tilak as an invincible hero and as the antagonist of the British power in India.

Role of Tilak in National Movement

Tilak's role in the Indian National Congress was that of an agitator. He wanted that the Congress should have its roots in the life of the populace. From 1905 to 1907 and from 1917 to 1920 he played a decisive job in the congress. He taught the gospel of self reliance and self-help at a time when some of the other leaders were mainly looking to Britishers sympathy and support. Tilak introduced extremist national sentiments in the Congress. The Congress so for was mainly middle class organisation. He attempted to bring it to the Congress the lower middle class groups and the ordinary people.

Tilak the Statesman

As one of the greatest makers of the modern India, Lokmanya has won undying fame. He was not only an agitator but was a statesman whose life work is the formation of the foundations of a strong country. Bal Gangadhar Tilak was an eminent politician and an all pervasive and exalted patriotism was the central theme of his life. The mission of Tilak's life was to rouse patriotic self-consciousness among populace of India. But he was not merely the prophet of an aggressive nationalism movement of India under British rule. He was also a leader who made enormous efforts to execute his ideas into concrete action. Hence, Tilak did not remain merely political intellectual but was a practical statesman of a high order. Tilak and his deeds are unique in several respects and for generations his memories will inspire Indians and freedom lovers all over the globe. In political life, Tilak was the Bhisma of Indian nationalism. He was an intellectual leader, a statesman and a moral hero for the nation.

Tilak's Social Philosophy

Tilak was a believer in the Advaita philosophy. He had a very comprehensive conception of Hinduism in his mind. In a speech of January 3, 1906, he said 'The term Sanatan Dharma shows that our religion is very old, as old as the olden times of human race itself. Vedic religion was the religion of the Aryans from ancient times. Entire Hindu religion is made up of different parts correlated to each other as so many daughters and sons of one great religion. If this idea is kept in view and if we try to unite the various sections it will be consolidated in a mighty force. Religion is an element in nationality. The word Dharma means a tie and comes from the root dhri, to bear or hold 'what is there to hold together'. To connect the soul with god, and man with man, dharma means our duties towards God and duties towards man. Hindu religion as such provides for a social as well as moral tie. Lokmanysa has given a broad definition of Hindu. According to him, a Hindu is one who accepts the authoritativeness of Vedas. A Hindu moulds his ways according to the injunctions of the Vedas the smritis and the puranas.

Tilak's Political Philosophy

Tilak's political philosophy has its roots both in the tradition of India as well as in some of the currents of contemporary western and legal contemplation. His key problem in life was the political liberation of India and there is an element of great realism in his political thoughts and outlook. He, however, was not a realist in the Hobbesian and Machiavellian sense of the term. Tilak was well-versed in Sanskrit philosophy and his political conceptions represent a blend of some of the dominant of Indian thought and the nationalistic and democratic ideas of the world.

The metaphysical assumptions of Bal Gangadhar Tilak influenced his political views. According to him, the metaphysics of non-dualism of the

Vedanta implied the political idea of natural right. Advaita taught him the supremacy of the concept of liberty. Liberty is the very life of the individual soul which Vedanta declares to be not separate from Almighty but identical with him. Liberty, according to Tilak, was a divine attribute. Liberty may be sum up with the autonomous power of creativism. Without liberty no moral and spiritual life is possible. Western imperialism kills the soul of a country and hence Lokmanya fought against the British Raj.

Tilak's Concept of Nationalism

Nationalism of Tilak was also influenced by the theories of western nations of national independence and self-determination. In the well-known trial speech of 1908, Tilak quotes with approval of John Stuart Mill's definition of nationality. In 1919 and 1920 he accepted the concept of self-determination of Wilsonian and pleaded for its application to India. Hence, Tilak's philosophy of nationalism was a synthesis of the vedantic ideal of the spirit as supreme liberty and the Mazzini, Edmund Burke, J.S. Mill and Woodrow Wilson conceptions of western nations. Because of his spiritual approach, Tilak regarded that swarajya was not merely a right but dharma.

Tilak as a Leader

As a leader, Tilak wanted to create a solid nationalistic following in Maharashtra and for the purpose he wanted to symbolise the permanent religious and historic traditions of the people. The Shivaji and the Ganapati festivals were the symbols of the rising symbolism in the State of Maharashtra and later on, to some extent, in other parts of India also. The Ganapathi unsaved was an old institution and is traditional in Maharastra. By inaugurating the Ganapthi festival, Tilak tried to bring nationalism to the masses. He regarded Shivaji as a vibhuti, in the language of Gita. A vibhuti is a man gifted with creative powers of divine nature. According to Tilak, national festivals provided opportunities of confraternity amongst the educated and uneducated multitude. Tilak proposes that nationalism is invisible and concrete entity but is a kind of sentiment, an idea, and in generating this idea the historical memories of the great personalities of a nation play a important role. Tilak had a systematic philosophy of nationalism.

He felt that the roots of Indian nationalism must be not with only intellectual appeals to the theories of the western liberal writers but in the sentiments and emotions of the Indian masses and hence he felt that the memories of Shivaji Maharaj would serve to reinvigorate nationalistic emotions of the common populace Shivaji was the symbol of the resentment and resistance of the people against oppression and injustice. Thus Tilak wanted to substantiate the nationalist movement in India by a strong cultural and religious revival of Hinduism.

Swaraj and Swadeshi Movements

Two important features in political philosophy of Tilak separated him from the moderate thinkers. First, unlike the moderates who argued for gradual introduction of democratic institutional in India, he insisted on immediate swaraj or self-rule. Tilak's concept of swaraj was incomplete in dependence but a government constituted by the Indian themselves that rules according to the wishes of the populace or their representatives. Similar to the British executive that decides on policies, impose and remove taxes and determine the allocation of public expenditure, people of India should have the right to run their own government and administration, to make laws, to appoint the administrators as well as to spend the tax revenue. The second dimension relates to the notion of the right of the populace to resist an authority that loses legitimacy.

As early as 1895, Lokamany had begun to preach the necessity for self-rule. He came to realise that self-rule or swaraj must precede meaningful social reform, that merely enduring basis for national unity and national self-respect must be national self-rule or so called swaraj. He had reminded the common people that Shivaji had recreated swaraj as the essential foundation of social and political liberty. His insistence on swaraj was fully consistent with his personal, social and political philosophy.

Programmes of Tilak

Tilak presented the nation with a threefold programme or techniques for effective practical and political action. The three principles were boycott, swadshi and national education. Boycott initially involved the refusal of the people to purchase British manufactured goods. It was started as a measure designed to bring economic pressure on the British business interests, both in India and abroad. Boycott progressively moved from the economic sphere into the political sphere. In 1906, at the Calcutta Congress, Tilak supported the swadeshi resolution and spelled out the economic basis of Indian nationalism. The swadeshi movement quickly became a movement of national regeneration: swadeshi was a practical application of love of nation.

Tilak and Swaraj

Swaraj became the reason and justification for the whole programme and movement led by Bal Gangadhar Tilak and other nationalists. He held that the attainment of swaraj would be great victory for Indian nationalism. He gave to Indian the mantra:' swaraj is the birth right of Indians. He defined swaraj or self-rule as rule of people instead of that of bureaucracy. With the co-operation of Annie Besant for pushing his ideal of swaraj forward he started Home Rule League in 1916. Tilak contemplated federal type of political structure under swaraj. He referred to the example of the American Congress and said that the government of India should keep it hands similar powers to exercise them through an impartial council for the correct implementation of his programme. Tilak urged the method of nonviolent passive resistance. Thus Tilak's method of action was democratic and constitutional. He had constructed practical objective. The swadeshi boycott movement in support of swaraj demand was an attempt at vindicating the rights of the populace to self administration and hence it used numerous techniques of political agitations as mass processions, big public assemblies, strikes, picketing etc, which have been followed by later leaders of India in their political national movements.

Tilak was one of the dominant political figures who gave to the people of India the first lessons in the consciousness of the right of swaraj. He enlightened the population of India into a political recognition of the general will of the nation. He has given us a theory of nationalism. Theory of nationalism of Tilak was fusion of the teachings of both western and eastern thinkers. Tilak was not only a nationalist leader with incredible political acumen. He himself represented a new wave of nationalist movement that created an automatic space for it by providing the most powerful and persuasive critique of moderate philosophy and articulating his nationalist ideology in language that was meaningful to those it was addressed.

References

1. All about Lokamanya Tilak. Madras: Ramaswamy Sastrulu & Sons, 1922.

2. Ahuja Ram. Social Problems in India. Jaipur: Rawat Publishers, 1999.

3. Appadorai A. Ed. Documents on Political Thought in Modern India. Vols. New Delhi: Oxford University Press, 1973, 2.

4. _____ Political Thought in India (400 B.C. - 1980). Delhi: Khama Publishers, 2002.

5. Argov Daniel. Moderates and Extremists in Indian National Movement. Bombay: Asia Publishing House, 1967.

6. Arti. Indian Nationalism and Tilak: A Critical Analysis. New Delhi: National Book Organisation, 1999.

7. Athalye DV. The Life of Lokamanya Tilak. Poona: Annasahib Chiploonkar, 1921.

8. Aurobindo Sri. The Human Cycle; the Ideal of Human Unity; War and Self-Determination. Pondicherry: Sri Aurobindo Ashram, 1977.

9. ____ Bande Mataram: Early Political Writings-1. Pondicherry: Sri Aurobindo Ashram, 1972, 1.

10. ____ Karmayogin: Early Political Writings-2. Pondicherry: Sri Aurobindo Ashram, 1972, 2.

11. ____ The Foundations of Indian Culture and the Renaissance in India, 14

12. Pondicherry: Sri Aurobindo Ashram, 1971.

13. Azad AK. India Wins Freedom. Calcutta: Orient Longmans, 1960.

14. Bakshi SR. Swaraj as Birth Right: Role of Tilak and Annie Besant. Delhi: Vista International Publishing House, 2006.

15. Bapat SV. Ed. Reminiscences and Anecdotes of Lokamanya Tilak. vols. Poona: S.V. Bapat, 1924-28, 3.

16. Bhat VG. Lokamanya Tilak: His Life, Mind, Politics and Philosophy. Poona: A Prakash Publication, 1956.

17. Brodov V. Indian Philosophy in Modern Time. Trans. Sergei Syrovatkin. Moscow: Progress Publishers, 1984. Brass, Paul R. The

Politics of India since Independence. Cambridge: Cambridge University Press, 1990.

18. Cashman Richard I. The Myth of Lokamanya: Tilak and Mass Politics in Maharashtra. Berkeley: University of California Press, 1975.

19. Chandra Ramesh. Ed. Globlisation, Liberalisation, Privatisation and Indian Polity. Vols. Delhi: Isha Books, 2004, 8.

20. Chattopadhyaya Debiprasad. Indian Philosophy. Delhi: People's Publishing House, 1972.

21. Chelysheva Irina. Ethical Ideas in the World Outlook of Swami Vivekananda, Lokamanya B.G. Tilak and Aurobindo Ghosh. Calcutta: Vostok, 1989.

22. Choudhary Sukhbir. Growth of Nationalism in India (1919-1929). New Delhi: Trimurti Publications, 1973.

23. Chousalkar Ashok S. Indian Idea of Political Resistance: Aurobindo, Tilak, Gandhi and Ambedkar. Delhi: Ajanta Publications, 1990.

24. Damle PR. Three Leaders: Tilak - Gokhale - Gandhi. Pune: Mrs. Kamalini Damle, 1962.

25. Das Hari Hara. Indian Political Thought. Jaipur: National Publishing House, 2005.

26. Das HH, Patro PSN. Indian Political Traditions. Bangalore: Sterling Publications, 1988.

27. Dasgupta SN. A History of Indian Philosophy. vols. Cambridge: Cambridge University Press, 1922-54, 5.

28. Desai AR. Social Background of Indian Nationalism. Bombay: Popular Prakashan, 1948.

29. Dubey SN. The Development of Political Thought in India (1885-1935). Delhi: ACME Publications, 1983.

30. Dutt R Palme. *India Today.* Rev. and enl. ed. Bombay: People's Publishing House, 1947.

31. Dutta Prabhat. Towards Good Governance and Sustainable Development. Kolkata: Das Gupta and Company, 2003.

32. Emmet Dorothy, Macintyre Alasdair. Ed. Sociological Theory and Philosophical Analysis. London: Macmillan & Co., 1970.

33. Fadia BL. Indian Government and Politics. Agra: Sahitya Bhawan Publications, 2007.

34. Gandhi MK. Democracy: Real and Deceptive. Comp. R.K. Prabhu. Ahmedabad: Navjivan Publication, 1961.

35. Ghaswalla Sorab. Lokmanya Tilak: Symbol of Swaraj. New Delhi: Rupa & Co., 2003.

36. Gokhale DV. Ed. The Tilak Case, Poona: The Printing Agency, 1916.

37. Gopal Ram. Lokamanya Tilak: A Biography. Bombay: Asia Publishing House, 1956.

38. Goel SL. Good Governance: An Integral Approach. New Delhi: Deep and Deep Publications, 2007.

39. Goyal OP. Modern Indian Political Thought. Delhi: Kitab Mahal, 1964.

40. _____ Political Thought of Gokhale. Allahabad: Kitab Mahal, 1965.

41. Grover Verinder. Ed. Bal Gangadhar Tilak, Political Thinkers of Modern India. New Delhi: Deep and Deep Publications, 1991, 4.

42. Gupta DC. Indian National Movement. Delhi: Vikas Publications, 1970.

43. Inamdar NR. Ed. Political Thought and Leadership of Lokmanya Tilak. New Delhi: Concept Publishing Company, 1983.

44. Jha MN. Modern Indian Political Thought: Ram Mohan Roy to Present Day. Meerut: Meenakshi Prakashan, 1975.

45. Jog NG. Lokamanya Bal Gangadhar Tilak. New Delhi: Indian Government Publications Division, 1970.

46. Kapoor Suneera. Sri Aurobindo Ghosh and Bal Gangadhar Tilak: The Spirit of Freedom. New Delhi: Deep and Deep Publications, 1990.

47. Kanetkar MJ. Tilak and Gandhi: A Comparative Sketch. Nagpur: M.J. Kanetkar, 1935.

48. Karandikar SL. Lokamanya Bal Gangadhar Tilak: The Hercules and Prometheus of Modern India. Poona: S.L. Karandikar, 1957.

49. Karmarkar DP. Bal Gangadhar Tilak: A Study. Bombay: Popular Book Depot, 1956.

50. Kashyap Subhash C. Blue Print of Political Reforms. Delhi: Shipra Publications, 2003.

51. _____ Ed. Eradication of Corruption and Restoration of Values. New Delhi: Sterling Publications, 2001.

52. Keer Dhananjay. Lokamanya Tilak: Father of the Indian Freedom Struggle. Bombay: Popular Prakashan, 1969.

53. Kelkar NC. Full and Authentic Report of the Tilak Trial. Bombay: The Indu Prakash Steam Press, 1908.

54. _____ Landmarks in Lokamanya's Life. Madras: Ganesan & Co., 1924.

55. _____ Life and Times of Lokamanya Tilak. Trans. D.V. Divekar. Madras: S. Ganesan, 1928.

56. _____ A Passing Phase of Politics. Poona: Shri Bharat Prakashan Karyalaya, 1925.

57. Khan MS. Tilak and Gokhale: A Comparrtive Study. New Delhi: Ashish Publishing House, 1992.

58. Kulkarni BR. Lokamanya Tilak's Metaphysics of Morals. Lokamanya. Tilak Memorial Lectures, Poona: University of Poona, 1973.

59. Kumar Ravinder. Western India in the Nineteenth Century: A Study in the Social History of Maharashtra. London: Routledge & Kegan Paul, 1968.

60. _____ Ed. Selected Documents of Lokamanya Bal Gangadhar Tilak (2880-1920). Vols. New Delhi: Anmol Publications, 1992, 4.

61. Kumar Vijender. Current Issues in Modern Political Thought. Jaipur: Pointer Publications, 2003.

62. Lal AK, Ahmad S. Sami. Ed. Social Change in Post-Independence India. Jaipur: Rawat Publications, 2001.

63. Mahajan Vidyadhar. Leaders of the Nationalist Movement. New Delhi: Sterling Publishers, 1975.

64. Malhotra SL. Social and Political Orientations of Neo-Vedantism: Study of the Social Philosophy of Vivekananda, Aurobindo, Bipin Chandra Pal, Tagore, Gandhi, Vinoba and Radhakrishnan. New Delhi: S. Chand & Co., 1970.

65. Majumdar RC. Ed. The History and Culture of the Indian People: Struggle for Freedom. Bombay: Bharatiya Vidya Bhavan, 1969.

66. _____ History of the Freedom Movement in India. Calcutta: Firma K.L.M. Private Ltd., 1977, 3.

67. Mehta VR. Ideology, Modernization and Politics in India. New Delhi: Manohar Publications, 1983.

68. Mittal KK. Materialism in Indian Thought. Delhi: Munshiram Manohar Lal Publications, 1974.

69. Mohanty DK. Indian Political Traditions: From Manu to Ambedkar. New Delhi: Anmol Publications, 1997.

70. Moore RJ. Ed. Tradition and Politics in South Asia. New Delhi: Vikas Publishing House, 1979.

71. Mukherjee SN. Ed. South Asian Affairs-2: The Movement for National Freedom in India. London: Oxford University Press, 1966.

72. Nevinson HW. The New Spirit in India. Delhi: Metropolitan Book Co., 1975.

73. Natarajan SA. Century of Social Reform in India. Bombay: Asia Publishing House, 1959.

74. Nehru JL. The Discovery of India. Calcutta: Asia Publishing House, 1947.

75. Pantham Thomas, Deutsh Kenneth L. Eds. Political Thought in Modern India. New Delhi: Sage Publications, 1986.

76. Parvate TV. Bal Gangadhar Tilak. Ahmedabad: Navajivan Publishing House, 1958.

77. Parel Anthony J. Ed. Gandhi: Freedom and Self-Rule. New Delhi: Vistaar Publications, 2002.

78. Pradhan GP, Bhagwat AK. Lokmanya Tilak: A Biography. Bombay: Jaico Publishing House, 1959.

79. Puri Harish K, Judge Paramjit S. Social and Political Movements. Jaipur: Rawat Publications, 2000.

80. Ramaiah A. Law for Dalit Rights and Dignity. Jaipur: Rawat Publications, 2007.

81. Radhakrishnan S. Indian Philosophy. 2nd ed. London: George Allen and Unwin, 1929, 1.

82. Ramaswami Aiyer CP. Biographical Vistas: Sketches of Some Eminent Indians. Bombay: Asia Publishing House, 1968.

83. Ray Sibnarayan. Ed. Gandhi, India and the World. Bombay: Nachiketa Publications, 1970.

84. Reisner IM, Goldberg NM. Eds. Tilak and the Struggle for Indian Freedom. New Delhi: People's Publishing House, 1966.

85. Reilly Benjamin. Democracy in Divided Societies: Electoral Engineering for Conflict Management. Cambridge: Cambridge

University Press, 2001.

86. Samagra Lokmanya Tilak. vols. Poona: Kesari Prakashan, 1974-76, 7.

87. Sapru RK. Administrative Theories and Management Thought. New Delhi: Prentice Hall of India Private Limited, 2006.

88. Sarhadi AS. Nationalism in India: The Problem. Delhi: Heritage Publishers, 1973.

89. Sathe Shanta. Lokmanya Tilak: His Social and Political Thoughts. Delhi: Ajanta Publications, 1994.

90. Seal Anil. The Emergence of Indian Nationalism: Competition and Collaboration in the Late Nineteenth Century. Cambridge: At the University Press, 1968.

91. Sharma Jyoti. Tilak and Gandhi: Perspectives on Religion and Politics. New Delhi: Gyan Publishing House, 2001.

92. Sharma NK. Lokamanya Tilak. New Delhi: Mahaveer & sons, 2007.

93. Sharma SR. Life and Works of Bal Gangadhar Tilak. Jaipur: Book Enclave, 2007.

94. Sharma Shri Ram. Freedom Movement (1857-1947). Delhi: B.R. Publishing Corporation, 1988.

95. Shay Theodore L. The Legacy of the Lokamanya: The Political Philosophy of Bal Gangadhar Tilak. Bombay: Oxford University Press, 1956.

96. Shrivastava Sudharani. Humanity and Human Rights. New Delhi: Commonwealth Publishers, 2004.

97. Singh SR. Nationalism and Social Reform in India. Delhi: Ranjit Printers and Publishers, 1968

98. Singh MK. Ed. Encyclopaedia of Great Indian Political Thinkers: Bal Gangadhar Tilak. New Delhi: Anmol Publications, 2008, 3.

99. Singh Nihar Nandan. Lokmanya Bal Gangadhar Tilak. New Delhi: Congress Centenary Celebration Committee, 1985.

100. A Step in the Steamer. Bombay: The National Bureau, 1918.

101. Tahmankar DV. Lokamanya Tilak: Father of Indian Unrest and Maker of Modern India. London: John Murry, 1956.

102. Terchek Ronald J. Gandhi: Struggling for Autonomy. New Delhi:

Vistaar Publications, 2000.

103. Tilak BG. The Arctic Home in the Vedas. Poona: Tilak Bros, 1956.

104. _____ The Orion, Or Researches into the Antiquity of the Vedass Poona: Tiiak Bros, 1925.

105. _____ His Writings and Speeches. Enl. ed. Madras: Ganesh & Co, 1919.

106. _____ Vedic Chronology and Vedanga jyotisha. New Delhi: Cosmo Publications.

107. _____ Srimad Bhagavadgita - Rahasya or karma-yoga-sastra. Trans. Sukthankar. 2nd ed. Poona: Tilak Bros, 1965.

108. Tiwari Vinod. Bal Gangadhar Tilak. Trans. Igen B. Delhi: Manoj Publications, 2008.

109. Varma SP. Modern Political Theory. New Delhi: Vikas Publishing House, 1999.

110. Varma VP. The Life and Philosophy of Lokamanya Tilak. Agra: Lakshmi Narain Agarwal, 1978.

111. _____ Modern Indian Political Thought. Agra: Lakshmi Narain Agarwal, 1961.

112. _____ Studies in Hindu Political Thought and its Metaphysical Foundations. 3rd ed. Delhi: Motilal Banarsidas, 1974.

113. Vidwans MD. Ed. Letters of Lokamanya Tilak. Poona: Kesari Prakashan, 1966.

114. Wolpert SA. Tilak and Gokhale: Revolution and Reform in the Making of Modern India. Berkeley: University of California Press, 1962.

115. Barber Benjamin R. Can Democracy Survive Globalisation? Government and Opposition: An International journal of Comparative Politics. 2007; 63(4):122-154.

116. Basu SK. The Two Interpretations of the Gita: Tilak's Karmayoga and Gandhi's Anasaktiyoga, Gandhi Marg. 1983; 5(6):315-29.

117. Bhatt Wasudha. The Crisis of Development: A Historical Critique from the Focal Point of Human Well-being. The Indian Journal of Political Science. 2007; 68(l):41-55.

118. Bhagwan Vishnu. Corruption and Good Governance. The Indian Journal of Political Science. 2007; 68(4):727-38.

119. Bharathi KS. Swadeshi and Globalization. Gandhi Marg. 2005; 27(1):59-73.

120. Biswas Prasenjit. Swaraj as a Human Value: A Gandhian Reading of Globalization. Gandhi Marg. 1999; 21(1):37-47.

121. Brandnock Robert. Economic Development in India. The Round Table. 1978; 272:325-32.

122. Brown D Mackenzie. The Philosophy of Bal Gangadhar Tilak: Karma vs. Jnana in the Gita Rahasya. Journal of Asian Studies. 1958; 17(2):197-206.

123. Chakravarty Anupama. Taking the Child from Factory to School. Democratic World. 1995; 24(13):19-21.

124. Diwakar RR. The Lokamanya and the Mahatma. Gandhi Marg. 1969; 16(3):188-195.

125. Dubashi Jay. Swadeshi and Globalisation. Janata. 1999; 54(1-5):37-43, 54.

126. Engineer Asghar Ali. Communal Riots. Janata. 2007; 61(49):11-15.

127. Gehlot NS. Towards Good Governance: A need for Political Reforms in India. Panjab journal of Politics. 2005; 29(2)127-143.

128. Ghosh Sekhar. Globalisation, Governance and the State: A View from the Third World. Indian Quarterly. 2007; 63(3):1-24.

129. Ghosh Sujan. The Second Generation of Democracy in India. West Bengal Political Science Review. 2005; 8(1-2):300-315.

130. Gopal SM. Globalisation: The Roots of Human Rights Violation. Janata. 2002; 57(34):9-12.

131. Jha Nalin Kant. Realising the Constitutional Vision: Road Blocks and Road Ahead. The Indian Journal of Political Science. 2005; 66(1):9-28.

132. Jha UK. Democracy in India: A Human Rights Perspective. Third Concept. 2002; 15(179):13-14.

133. Jose PK. Gandhi and Tilak: Values in Conflict. Gandhi Marg. 1989; 2(1):42-61.

134. _____ Responsive Co-operation and Non-Co-operation: Strategies in Strife. Gandhi Marg. 1990; 20(3):317-328.

135. Kalbag Chaitanya. The Abridgement of Individual Liberty. Janata. 2008; 63(1):13-16.

136. Kapoor Suneera. The Idea of Nationalism: A Study in the Political

Thought of Tilak, Aurobindo and Gandhi. Gandhian Perspectives. 1996; 9(1):29-37.

137. _____ Truth and Non-Violence: A Study in the Ideas of Tilak and Gandhi. New Quest. 1998; 129:149-53.

138. Kapoor Suneera, Chauhan Abha. Concept of Swaraj: A Study in the Political Ideas of Tilak and Gandhi. Third Concept. 2005; 18(216):10-15.

139. Khare Vijay. Human Rights in India: Child Labour. Third Concept. 2002; 16(187):31-33.

140. Mahajan Gurpreet. Civil Society and its Avatars: What Happened to Freedonn and Democracy? Economic and Political Weekly. 1999; 34(20):1188-96.

141. Malla N. Swaraj, Science and Civilization. Gandhi Marg. 1981; 3(6):345-53.

142. Mander Harsh. The State of the Nation. Janata. 2008; 63(1):5-7.

143. Mehta Sanat. Present Day Indian Politics. Janata. 2007; 62(1):11-15.

144. Morse Jane. Forced Labour, a Growing Problem. Janata. 2007; 62(27):15.

145. Mukherjee Uma, Mukherjee Haridas. The Alleged Uniqueness of Indian Freedom Movement. Modern Review. 1962; 112:103-107.

146. Mukhopadhyay Arun. Child Labour: A Problem Structural to Economy. Socialist Perspective. 2002; 30(1-2):1-6.

147. Naidu Ashok. Secularism Re-Examined. The Indian Journal of Political Science. 2007; 68(3):607-614.

148. Naidu MV. Globalisation: Threat or Promise? Gandhi Marg. 1999; 21(1):21-25.

149. Naidu Y Gurappa. Globalisation and its Impact on Indian Society. The Indian Journal of Political Science. 2006; 67(1):65-76.

150. Nayar Kuldeep. Is Press Independent? Janata. 2007; 62(29):5-6.

151. Parida Pradeep Kumar. Globalisation, Relative Deprivation and Terrorism: An Analysis. India Quarterly. 2007; 63(4):122-154.

152. Parsa Venkat. Rise in Farmer Suicides in Gujrat. Janata. 2007; 62(39):7.

153. Parvate TV. Tilak and Gandhi: Conceptions and Misconceptions.

Gandhi Marg. 1967; 2(4):351-64.

154. Pradhan Rudra Prakash. Rural Poverty Alleviation: India's Experiences and Needed Strategy. India Quarterly. 2006; 62(3):152-188.

155. Pradhan SP, Bhagwat AK. Lokamanya Tilak: The Politician and the Reformer. Quest. 1956; 2(1):43-48.

156. Paul MC. Dowry as a Symbol of Women's Subordination in India. Social Action. 1992; 42(3):305-313.

157. Raj SR. Swadeshi in the Context of Globalization: A Grassroot Development Perspective. Gandhi Marg. 2000; 22(1):77-83.

158. Rajarajan R. Secularism in Indian Politics: Theory and Practice. The Indian journal of Political Science. 2007; 68(2):403-412.

159. Ramajayam. Caste and Religion in India. Third Concept. 2007; 21(248):25-30.

160. Sacher Rajinder. Secular Democracy and Composite Culture. Janata. 2008; 63(1):12-16.

161. Sakthivel P, Sivakumar R. Declining Moral Values and Politics in India. Third Concept. 2007; 21(248):37-40.

162. Sankaranarayan P. Education for all. Janata. 2007; 62(46):14-15.

163. _____ Always an Untouchable. Janata. 2007; 62(48):3-5.

164. _____ India Shining and Hindustan Waning. Janata. 2007; 62(49):7.

165. Sarkar Sumita. Beggary in Urban India: Conflict and Challenges of Human Development. Social Action. 2007; 57(1):44-55.

166. Sekar Hemavathi. Globalisation of Service Activities: Opportunities and Challenges for India. India Quarterly. 2006; 62(3):1-22.

167. Sethi Jajneswar. Political Corruption in India. Third Concept. 2008; 22(254):28-31.

168. Shanker Kripa. Poverty in India. Janata. 2007; 62(40):20-21.

169. Sharma CL. State of Democracy in India. The Indian Journal of Political Science. 2006; 67(1):9-20.

170. Sharma Vijay. Gandhian Vision of Democracy. Third Concept. 2008; 22(254):11-19.

171. Shekhawat VS. Corruption in India: An Exercise in Perpetuity. The Indian Journal of Political Science. 2005; 66(2):395-404.

172. Shukla SP. Globalisation: Life and Livelihoods. Janata. 2008; 63(11):13-15.

173. Singh Ranbir. Corruption in Indian Politics. Punjab Journal of Politics. 2003; 27(2):69-86.

174. Singh Avtar. Child Labour Problems and Prospects: Socio-Legal Measures. Social Action. 2004; 54(4):396-410.

175. Singh Ishwar. Constitution of India as an Instrument of Economic Growth and Social Justice. The journal of Parliamentary Information. 1993; 39(1):113-123.

176. Sinha Kewal Prasad. The Role of Free Press in Democratic State." journal of Political Studies. 1984; 17(1):56-60.

177. Skinner Quentin. Meaning and Understanding in the History of Ideas. History and Theory. 1969; 8:3-53.

178. Surana Pannalal. Violence - Great Challenge to Civil Society. Janata. 2007; 62(1):16.

179. I'hakurdas Frank. In Defence of Social Equality. Journal of Political Studies. 1976; 9(1):40-65.

180. T'ilak BG. The Evils of Child Marriage. Mahratha. 1881; 1(22):1-8.

181. Unisa Sayeed, Bhagat RB. Child Marriages in India: Is Ameena an Exception? Social Action. 1992; 42(1):86-88.